KEDARKANTHA WHISPERS

VAIBHAV DEVANGKUMAR VAIDYA

Contents

Preface   *v*

About the Author   *vii*

Acknowledgements   *ix*

The Transformative Power of Kedarkantha   *xi*

1. Work & Wanderlust: Solo Trek   1

2. Freedom Quest: Work To Himalayan Bliss   4

3. Mussoorie Discovery: Dalai Hill And Snow   9

4. Journey's Dawn: Mussoorie To Sankri   17

5. Juda Ka Talab: Mythical Ascent   32

6. Fox Encounter: A Night Of Silent Shadows   52

7. Summit Dreams And Snowman Smiles   57

8. Whispers Of Kedarkantha: A New Beginning   71

Preface

Welcome to the enthralling odyssey through the mesmerizing landscapes of Kedarkantha—a journey that transcends the realms of a mere trek and ventures into the heart and soul of the mighty Himalayas. As you immerse yourself in the unfolding chapters, be prepared to traverse the snow-clad paths, witness the dance of elusive foxes, and experience the profound beauty that only nature's canvas can paint.

This book serves as a chronicle, capturing the essence of Kedarkantha in every step, breath, and heartbeat. Beyond a travel narrative, it encapsulates the profound connection between the trekker and the towering peaks, between companions and the serene solitude of the mountains. Each paragraph is a testament to the resilience of the human spirit amid the breathtaking backdrop of snow-laden peaks and the untamed wild.

Embarking on the trek to Kedarkantha is not merely a physical journey; it is a spiritual sojourn, a pilgrimage to the sacred heart of the Himalayas. From the whispers of snowflakes to encounters with elusive foxes, from the comforting presence of a loyal canine companion to the magical hues of a mountain sunset—these moments are not just recounted; they are relived.

The frozen expanse of Juda Ka Talab becomes a metaphor for life's challenges, and the trek, an allegory for the arduous climb towards our aspirations. As you journey through these pages, may you discover not just the external landscapes but also the inner landscapes of self-discovery and reflection.

Trekking is a metaphor for life's journey, an ascent towards the peaks of our dreams. So, tighten your metaphorical backpack, brace for the uphill climb, and let the stories within these pages guide you through the snow-covered trails of Kedarkantha.

Here's to the adventure that awaits—a journey through the heart of Kedarkantha!

About The Author

Meet Vaibhav Vaidya, a distinguished HR professional and the creative mind behind this book. This serves as his second venture into the world of writing, showcasing his dedication to sharing valuable experiences and insights.

Outside of his professional commitments, Mr. Vaidya is a passionate traveller, with a special affinity for Uttarakhand. His wanderlust knows no bounds, spanning the heights of mountains to the expanses of beaches. Embracing the spirit of solo travel, he maximizes the richness of each journey.

Balancing his role as an Assistant Manager - HR in a private company, Mr. Vaidya consistently carves out time for his explorations, recognizing that travel is a crucial aspect of a fulfilling life. Embark on this literary and adventurous journey with him.

Connect with Vaibhav Vaidya through the following social media channels:

- YouTube : Being HR
- LinkedIn: www.linkedin.com/in/vvaidya002/
- Website: www.beinghrprofessional.com
- Instagram: www.instagram.com/vvaidya17

Acknowledgements

I would like to extend my sincere gratitude to all those who played a vital role in making both this incredible journey and the creation of this book possible. A special thank you goes out to my parents for their unwavering support; without them, this book would not have seen the light of day.

I also want to express my deep appreciation to my friends—Vishal, Prabhu, Sunil, Dhruv, Krishna, and Mansi—for being my pillars of strength throughout this endeavor.

A heartfelt acknowledgment to my colleagues and boss at the office—Bhavesh Sir, Sanket Sir, Ruzul, Sreejith, and Hitesh—for their constant motivation and encouragement.

My heartfelt gratitude to my father, Devang Vaidya, for his wonderful words. Wishing you a delightful journey!

I extend my heartfelt gratitude to my mother, Diksha Vaidya, for her meticulous proofreading that has enhanced the precision and polish of the words within these pages. Lastly, but most importantly, I want to convey my appreciation to my dear and supportive sister, Krishita.

Krishita, believe me, once you complete your board exams, we will embark on a trek together.

With profound gratitude,

Vaibhav Devangkumar Vaidya

The Transformative Power Of Kedarkantha

Dear Readers,

If you find yourself engrossed in the pages of this book, it's safe to assume that you share an affinity for mountains. Within these lines, I'd like to impart a perspective that extends beyond the physical aspects of trekking and mountain climbing; it delves into the realm of mental well-being.

The journey of ascending a mountain is not merely a test of your physical prowess; it's a profound exploration of your mental fortitude. When your mind is resilient, there's an unstoppable force propelling you forward.

Kedarkantha is no ordinary mountain peak; it holds the extraordinary ability to liberate you from negativity, tensions, and worries. Venturing here is not just a quest for altitude; it's a sojourn that weaves together indelible memories, introduces you to remarkable individuals, and imparts invaluable lessons that no classroom can encapsulate.

As you navigate the narrative ahead, consider the mountains not just as majestic landscapes but as metaphors for the challenges and triumphs that shape the human spirit. Embrace the transformative power of Kedarkantha, and let the journey etch its mark on your soul.

To view all the photos and videos from this journey, check out our Instagram page, named "Kedarkantha Whispers."

Happy reading and, perhaps, even happier trekking!

Best regards,
Vaibhav Devangkumar Vaidya

CHAPTER ONE

WORK & WANDERLUST: SOLO TREK

There is a straightforward guideline that states that you must get your managers' permission before making trip plans. I had enough of working nonstop for almost three weeks without a single break. I was employed by a power distribution firm as an HR specialist. I was requested to do an HR perspective audit as part of an international audit that my firm was going through. I was putting in long hours of effort to meet my goals. The audit itself went pretty well, but before to it, I had planned a single excursion.

I began traveling alone in October 2021.Few of my close friends and relatives believed that I had gone insane and was emotionally unstable, but they had never witnessed my side of enjoyment. Going on a solo trip where you can do whatever you want. You make good friends and are well-versed in the real world. Furthermore, these solo trips allow me to reflect on myself. Thanks to my parents for always allowing me to do so (despite my begging), but yes, as a human resources professional, I have strong persuasion skills that have come in handy. I was more eager to return to the mountains of Uttarakhand after my first solo trip there.

I decided to go on one more trip in February 2022, during the audit preparation process. My colleagues and bosses were pleased to see me working so hard on weekends and holidays, but they were unaware that I was working not for the purpose of auditing but to create Compensatory Off that could be used during my leave because when you work for a private organization, you have limited leave. I had finally booked my trip to Kedarkantha before three days of auditing. I had no money at the time, and yes, my parents and the stock market helped me plan it. During that time, my YouTube channel also gave me money, which helped me book train tickets and pay for the trek. After 5 hours of YouTube research, I finally decided to book my trek with Himalayan Hikers because they were very affordable. I had no idea what trekking was or what a summit was. What were the difficulties?

I had one main goal: I wanted to go on a trek. I wasn't sure whether to choose the Kedarkantha trek or the Brahmatal trek. Kedarkantha sounded more challenging, so I picked that one. Everything was set, and I bought the tickets. My parents agreed. The only thing left was approval from my Manager HR and General Manager HR. This was the toughest part. My boss was cool, but getting approval from the General Manager of Human Resources was risky. I planned to ask for leave approval after the audit. I was ready for the audit, not worried about it, but concerned about my general manager approving my leave. However, things turned out differently.

The audit was extremely successful, and I requested leave, which was granted by the General Manager. I felt like I was on cloud seven. This contentment was priceless. On the same evening, my mother and I went to Decathlon to stock up on supplies for our trip. My parents were tense, an it was widespread as climbing a mountain is not without danger. It's not a walk on the beach. At the same time, my mother was preparing a special meal for me. She bought a few energy bars. Not only that, but I discovered that there is a tower issue at that location, so we bought a new simcard as well.

My aunt was so excited about it that she made a camphor box out of threads for me to wear around my neck during the trek. There will be less oxygen at higher altitudes, and she made three camphor thread boxes for me. This gesture made me so happy. Both excitement and nervousness were present. Excited to try something new, but nervous if I fail.

CHAPTER TWO

FREEDOM QUEST: WORK TO HIMALAYAN BLISS

Finally, I'll be traveling today. I went to work with a 24 carat smile. The finest part of working is knowing that you don't have to work for 10 days starting tomorrow. This is the biggest mental relief that a person can ever obtain. Clear your inbox and workstation. There was a lot of anticipation for this trip to begin. I was even happier because I knew there would be almost no network available in the region during my journey, which meant no calls, no internet, just me and nature.

At the same time, I was concerned about how my parents might reach me. My mother, in particular, would be concerned, but thanks to me, I had previously purchased one spare simcard for it. I actually felt horrible since there was no one in my team when I handed over responsibility for my job to my boss at the last minute. However, my manager was really supportive of the situation. Going home from the workplace felt so good because when you travel, you should not carry any work burdens with you. since the fact is that you can't hike while responding to emails since you'll miss the scenery.

While riding my bike, I was wondering about how I will be able to travel and handle all of these costs; the answer was because my parents supported me. Since coming from a middle-class household, traveling is a luxury, and trekking is an ultra-luxurious experience. Parents encourage us since they, too, want to do the same on their trip, but they were stymied by walls of responsibilities; yet, they never grumbled because they were mature. They enabled and supported me just because they desired to live their lives through me. I arrived home thinking about all of this. My mother was waiting for me to give me a lot of instructions (typical mother worldwide).

While writing this book, I am 28 years old and travel regularly; she still gives me advice, and I am confident that even if I lived to be 100, she would not stop. That is the joy of parenting. She was offering me all kinds of advice, such as "if you can't walk and climb so much, don't push yourself too hard; it's better to come back." She provided medication for fever, cold and cough, and high mountain altitude sickness. Now begins the difficult task of packing my suitcase (rucksack).

I knew I wasn't supposed to bring excess luggage because it would be tough to carry and walk with. So I attempted to pack less items, but being from a Gujarati family, how can we bring fewer luggage? My luggage may have weighed close to 20 Kgs. I'm guessing that 15 KGs were food. We can survive without everything, but not without food. I finally hired a cab to the railway station and was waiting for it. My father approached me and just said, "Enjoy your Journey." Wow, those words meant a lot to me.

After arriving at the railway station, I discovered that my RAC ticket had been confirmed and that I was going to get a whole berth to sleep in. I was overjoyed to learn this because sharing a berth would have been a major issue because the journey was longer than 24 hours and I needed to get some sleep and rest. The adventure had finally begun. The nicest thing about Indian railway is that there is no privacy in second class trains; you either ignore the person seated next to you or communicate with them. It was midnight, and everyone was sleeping, so I decided to sleep as well.

I was concerned about thefts, so I carried a little bag containing my phone and money. I used to sleep with one hand in the bag strip so that no one could simply steal it. Alarms are not required when traveling on Indian trains. It was 7:00 a.m., when food vendors began to appear in our compartment, offering chai, coffee, idli sambhar, and even pavbhaji. I was simply wondering who would eat Pav Bhaji at 7:00 a.m., but you can't anticipate people. There were just a few people who had bought it. I wasn't in the mood to eat anything, so I opted to simply sit and enjoy the sight from my window seat.

Trains are still not available everywhere in India. We were traveling through Rajasthan in the afternoon. Two gentlemen joined my cabin when the train stopped at a small station. Surprisingly, there was uncertainty between those two gentlemen and their families because they all had the same ticket. I was surprised at how this was feasible. Indian Railways are quite adept at allocating confirmed tickets and how this might happen. After about 20 minutes of misunderstanding, I decided to assist them in resolving it because the ticket checker had not yet arrived.

I had requested the gentleman to show me the ticket, and while the seat number and coach number were correct, as was the train number, the date was wrong. The date was of previous day. They had forgotten to check the date. People are sometimes so rushed that they overlook the date part. When they realized this, they decided to move towards unreserved coach. Two young men boarded our train from a small town station in the late afternoon. Those men did not have any reservation. They addressed the ticket checker, who assisted them in obtaining a reservation against the standard penalty of boarding a reserved coach.

Surprisingly, the ticket checker asked the young guy how many persons in total as he had to deduct the penalty , one of men said three, but in reality, they were only two. I was perplexed since I hadn't seen the third individual yet. The ticket checker inquired about the third individual. The man took out a Funerary Urn (Asthi Kalash) from his luggage and showed it to him. His father had died before a day, and his burial urn was being transported to Haridwar for rituals. He asked the ticket checker to make a ticket for this Funerary Urn containing his father's ashes, but it was clearly not feasible, and ticket checker said no.

This is what makes travel more educational. My country's people are so lovely that they desire a ticket for a Funerary Urn. They are linked to emotions. Finally, the sun sank in the west, and so did my vitality. I tried to sleep but was unable to do so. My train was approaching Delhi, and I was bored, so I decided to take a seat and listen to a few songs. A 35-40 year middle age lady was sitting two rows ahead of me. She noticed that I was the only one who wasn't sleeping in the coach and approached me, asking if she may sit near me.

Her station was only one hour away, and she was worried about falling asleep and missing the station. I assured her it was alright to sit. We started talking about traveling, and I found out that she is a teacher with a 9-year-old son. She was describing how life is unpredictable. In COVID-19, she had lost her husband. Her husband was a doctor, and she was having difficulties raising a child, but she did not give up. She resolved to provide a bright future for her child. She is a teacher in a private school in Delhi.

Schools in Delhi pay highly. Her child was in Rajasthan, and she used to travel there every weekend simply to see her child. She was working so hard for the child. She wants her son to be a doctor like his father. If women want to, they can do great things. She had not worked for 15 years after her marriage, but owing to her husband's untimely death, she chose to restart her profession. She was doing fine just now. It was a fantastic chat with that lady, and neither of us realized we had been talking for an hour. She bid good bye when our train departed from station.

I tried sleeping again, and this time I was successful. When I woke up early in the morning, it was Roorkee. The train's final stop was at Haridwar, and I was simply hoping to arrive on time. Because I had a connecting train from Haridwar to Dehradun with a two-hour stopover. Fortunately, my train arrived on schedule, and I arrived at Haridwar Railway Station. I'd been here a few times before, so I was aware that I'd need to take a covid test to leave the station, but happily, I'd taken a booster dose, so I was exempted.

CHAPTER THREE

Mussoorie Discovery: Dalai Hill and Snow

Upon my arrival at Haridwar, I found myself faced with a decision. I could either opt to bide my time for the next two hours, awaiting my train, and then endure a 1:30-hour journey to Dehradun. Alternatively, I could venture towards the bus stop situated opposite the railway station and board a bus bound for Dehradun, with an anticipated travel time of 1:30 hours. Opting for the latter, I embarked on the initial leg of my adventure by bus.

Making my way to the bustling bus terminal, fortune favored me as I discovered that a bus en route to Dehradun was on the brink of departure. Swiftly seizing the opportunity, I boarded the bus, feeling a sense of gratitude for the timely connection. The serendipitous encounter with the departing bus marked the auspicious commencement of my journey, leaving me with a profound sense of fortune for having caught that particular conveyance.

I intended to spend the day at Dehradun and then travel to Mussoorie. While sitting on the window seat, admiring the surroundings, I had the idea to remain in Mussoorie. My journey to Kedarkantha was about to begin the next morning from Dehradun. Since I knew that our bus would only travel the Mussoorie route, I phoned my trekking organizer and asked if he could pick me up from Mussoorie the next morning. He replied in the affirmative. I felt like I had won the lottery since I could now visit Mussoorie. I would be able to sleep for a few more hours.

Uttarakhand's capital city is Dehradun. We encountered heavy traffic as we approached the city, but my bus managed to drop me off near the city center. I needed to board a bus to Mussoorie after arriving in Dehradun, so I need to headed to the Dehradun Railway terminal, since the bus terminal is immediately outside the railway station. I grabbed a tuk tuk (Autorickshaw) for ten rupees and arrived at Dehradun Bus Station. There was a long que for the Mussoorie bus at the bus terminal. I learned that the next bus would arrive in 2 hours and that I would have to wait another 2-3 hours for my turn. A cab stop is located near the bus terminal. I went there to inquire about the rates. The cab fare was 1600 rupees, which I refused to pay. I informed the taxi stand proprietor that I was leaving. I planned to stay simply in Dehradun. The driver of the cab invited me to return on the way back and advised me to use a shared taxi, which would only cost 400 rupees. I was the only one on that taxi stand at the time, but the proprietor promised me that additional people will arrive in a few minutes.

Fortunately, 3 college students were on their way to Mussoorie stopped there to inquire about taxis, and the proprietor advised that the group go together. We were all fine because it was affordable. We all paid our fees and began our trek. From loud metropolitan traffic to the breathtaking mountains. The journey was breathtaking. It was fascinating to look out the windows and see Deodar, Oak, and Pine trees. The trip's highlight was seeing monkeys everywhere. Our driver was driving so quietly that I had no idea we had arrived at Mussoorie in just over an hour.

There was a large lane of traffic as we approached Mussoorie. Mussoorie is one of India's most picturesque hill stations. From December to February, there is a good likelihood of snowfall in Mussoorie, which is one of the reasons visitors visit. Not only that, but Mussoorie is well-known for filming films such as Kabir Singh, Kashmir Files, Krishna Cottage, and more. Our driver had dropped us off at the Mussoorie Chowk gate. The beauty of this location was that you could see the entire city from here. Nearby, there are numerous lodges, hotels, and restaurants. There was a gurdwara nearby, so I chose to stay there. I went to the Gurdwara and asked if there were any open rooms, and I got one for 500 rupees. I chose this location because my bus had been scheduled to pick me up at Mussoorie Chowk the next day, and it was just around 250 meters from the Gurdwara.

After checking into the room. I decided to take a break and then tour Mussoorie. The room was really spacious. I just took a shower and then began to consider where I should go. I decided to visit Company Garden first. I went to Chowk to inquire about Scotty rental. Because it was vacation season, they were charging 800-1000 rupees for a single day, which I thought was expensive. I had just checked the distance on the map and it was about 4 kilometers, so I decided to walk. It took over 45 minutes to arrive at the company garden. In the company garden, you can view a variety of trees, plants, and an artificial waterfall. But there was one thing that was the most beautiful part of visiting the company garden, and that was that there had been an unexpected snowfall over there before a week, and there was a portion of the snow that had not yet melted. This was the first time I had seen real snow. Even though there was less snow, it was still beautiful. It looked like a white bedsheet draped over little rose plants. I stood there over for atleast 15 minutes, staring at it like a small kid.

I was hungry, and there was a restaurant in the business garden. I made the decision to go there and eat something. I got a soup as well as the famous aloo Partha (my all-time favourite), which was both tasty and hot.

I wondered,where should I go next and I decided to go to a Tibetan Buddhist temple because I had never been to one before and wanted to learn more about them. It was over 3 kilometers from Company Garden, and I had decided to go there. So I started walking from the company garden to the Buddhist temple. It took me around 30 minutes to get there. Sadly, the temple was closed. According to the locals, the temple has been closed for many months, but there is another spot to explore, Dalai Lama Hill, which is very close to the temple.

To get to the top of the hills, you must walk for around 10-15 minutes. The Dalai Hills in Mussoorie lie approximately 400 meters from the Tibetan temple in Mussoorie's Happy Valley. Dalai Hills is one of the most majestic and stunningly picturesque spots in Mussoorie.

It will transport you away from little houses. There were various street food vendors offering Maggie and momos. When it comes to Maggie, you can't say no, so I opted for to have one. While ascending the mountain, you will notice numerous magnificent Buddhist flags. The flags are always arranged in the following order: blue, white, red, green, yellow. Blue signifies the sky, white represents the air, red represents fire, green represents water, and yellow represents earth. All five colors together represent balance. After reaching the top, I discovered a massive sculpture of Lord Buddha.

The Dalai Hills gives you a bird's eye view of the gigantic Garhwal Himalayan Range of Uttarakhand. The Dalai Hills is a very serene and tranquil place for all those who seek to experience the handsomeness and pleasantness of the hill station of Mussoorie.

Dalai Hills lies just above the Lal Bahadur Shashtri Academy. On a clear day you can gaze at some really captivating view of the greater Himalayas from here. Dalai Hills is also a treat to trekking buffs. There are a number of treks that go from the Dalai Hills, passing by thick forests rich in flora and fauna. When heading off to Dalai hills and if you plan to go for a trek do take some snacks along with you as you may be weary after a bit of a steep walk. But do not pollute the place and carry your waste back with you, do not mess the place, do not exploit the area. I took a few photographs and then decided to leave. I wanted to explore more of Mussoorie.

I felt very tired after reaching down. I wanted to go to the Gunhill ropeway, which was over 5 kilometers away from Dalai Hill. I was simply praying for a ride when I was approached by a local who was traveling the same way. He offered me a lift, which was quite calming. He worked in a government department. We were talking about the Covid crisis, and I was startled to learn that it had affected so many individuals. He was talking about his friends and family members who died as a result of COVID-19. For everyone, the Covid-19 time was one of the worst. He was talking about his duties during Covid-19 and how he worked for people all hours of the day and night. During the covid-19, he made numerous contributions. As a government employee with responsibilities in vaccination clinics and hospitals, he did not return home for months as a precaution.

He dropped me off near to the shopping road. I started walking to the ropeway ticket counter, only to find myself in yet another huge que. Fortunately, I was able to obtain round-trip tickets for about 75 rupees. As a single person, I immediately obtained a seat in the cabin and we were on our way to the gunhill.

Said to be an extinct volcano, the Gun Hill is the second-highest point in Mussoorie, situated at an altitude of 2024 meters. The scene from the top of this hill is a panoramic view of the snow-clad Himalayan ranges right beside the widespread Doon Valley and a full view of the hill station of Mussoorie. The Gun Hill, located 400 ft above the Mall Road, is a popular attraction, especially amongst the photographers and nature lovers.

The highlight of Gun Hill is the ropeway which provides a scenic view of the Himalayan ranges. The hill was named so because of the presence of a gun at these hills during the pre-independence days. The gun was fired during the day to enable people to adjust their watches during those days. The trip provides a bird's-eye perspective of the neighboring Himalayan mountains, including Shrikanta, Pithwara, and Bunderpunch, as well as colorful wildflowers.

It is also an excellent opportunity to picture the natural beauty that surrounds you. In reality, one can get off the ropeway somewhere in the middle for a few minutes to simply take in the scenery. On a clear day, it is often possible to see Gangotri through a telescope from Gun Hill.

After arriving in Gunhill, there were only a few gaming shops and restaurants (I would not recommend eating anything). I decided to go down after spending half an hour. There was no que while going down. I had quickly gotten into the cable car, and we were on our way down. It was extremely delightful to watch the Mussoorie valley.

After arriving at the Jhula ghar. I decided to walk through the mall road. I visited Mussoorie's well-known Cambridge Book Shop. It was Saturday, and every Saturday, the famous author Mr. Ruskin Bond would visit this book shop and met his fans. I immediately went to that shop in the hopes of seeing him, but when I arrived, I discovered that he had stopped coming because of his ill health was not good. I hope he recovers quickly.

I was walking along the mall road after leaving the shop. There are a lot of street vendors. I came across a tattoo artist. I despise tattoos but decided to have one (temporary tattoo). The person charged me 100 rupees and I selected a design of Lord Shiva. He drew one, and it was the worst thing I'd ever seen. He promised me that the tattoo will be there for at least 15 days, however it just lasted a few hours.

I started to look around further, and then I came across a jacket vendor. He was selling down jackets at a very reasonable price, so I bought two for my mother and father. The best aspect about these street vendors was that they now accepted UPI payments. I didn't want to use cash because I would need it during the trek.

After purchasing the jacket, I noticed a nearby chocolate shop. My mother enjoys chocolate, so I decided to buy her some candy, marshmallows, dark chocolate, and milk chocolate. When I told the shop owner that I was buying it for my mother, he offered me a few candies for free.

After a few minutes of strolling near the Gurdwara, I came to a restaurant. This restaurant's biggest feature was that it was on two levels and that you could view the entire Mussoorie from your table. I had a vegetarian meal with soup and it was delicious.

Then I decided to take a little walk on mall road after dinner. It was around 8 p.m., and you could see the entire Dehradun city light from the road. It was breathtaking. By 08:30, I had returned to my room and called my mother to tell her about my trip to Mussoorie. I decided to go to bed at 9:00 p.m. I set an alarm for 6:00 a.m. It had been a long day for me, and I fell asleep as soon as I got into bed.

CHAPTER FOUR

Journey's Dawn: Mussoorie to Sankri

Finally, the day had come for my trip journey to kick off. I woke before my alarm went on. I've never used an alarm clock to wake up in my life. I used to wake up before time. I believe it is a blessing for me. I quickly took a hot shower and dressed. There was only one problem now: I had purchased a few items the day earlier but had not stowed them in my backpack bag. Because I had limited space, I had to take everything out of my rucksack and repack it. I made it somehow. I had checked out of the room and needed to eat something, so I headed to Mussoorie Chowk and wondered where I should go for breakfast. I went to the newly opened Tea Shop and ordered a tea and a biscuit packet. It was 6:30 a.m., and it was getting freezing over there. I took off my hand glove to open the biscuit packet. It was so cold in the morning, I felt like my fingers were freezing as I opened the packet.

While sipping tea and enjoying the weather. I saw a dog watching me and sniffing around. He desired to consume the biscuits. Anyway, I didn't want to eat them so I gave those biscuits to that dog. After that, I had an aloo partha. While eating aloo partha, I received a call from the tour organizer informing me that the bus will arrive in 20-25 minutes. I hurriedly finished my breakfast and waited for the bus to arrive. I was enjoying the cool temperature and the sun. I went for a walk and looked out at the gorgeous valley from the Chowk. Meanwhile, my driver called to say he had arrived at the chowk. The Mussoorie Chowk is usually a fairly crowded area because it is a popular route to numerous spiritual and hiking destinations. It was a Mini Bus, not a bus. I wanted to keep my luggage in the trunk or on the top of the bus, but there was a lengthy line of cars and buses over there, so my driver suggested I keep my luggage on the bus's last empty seat.

Entering the bus, seeing the unfamiliar faces of the folks who would be my hiking companions for the next four days. I chose the last second seat because it was the sole accessible window seat. A middle-aged set of three people sat across from me. I smiled at them and introduced myself. I discovered they were from Madurai. Madurai is a lovely city in Tamil Nadu. I visited there in 2015. As a result of our discussion, I learned that they work for the State Bank of India. Sarvanan was the most active of the three members. My birthplace is Coimbatore, Tamil Nadu, and I had a few roots there, so I could speak a few Tamil words. They were delighted to see me. While we were talking about this, I noticed a beautiful waterfall outside my window. Kempty Falls, a massive fall with somersaults of the streams before striking the bottom, is the most popular and one of the oldest tourist destinations near Mussoorie. Kempty Falls, were first discovered before 150 years by a British man, it is the most fascinating picnic destination area nearby Mussoorie at a distance of 15 kilometers.

Our bus driver had granted us a 5-minute break just a few kilometers after Kempty Falls. It was only a short pause because the route was full of zigzag roads, and the next route would be the same. As all of us aboard the bus had been traveling for the past 2-3 days, it would be tough for us to continue on this path. So our driver promised that he would take at least 4-5 breaks. Our bus was parked near an open landscape area for our first break. On the opposite side, we could see plain mountains. There were few waterfalls on those mountains. Small houses can be seen in the valley if you look down. From above, those houses will look like matchboxes. During my time off, I met other participants of our journey, including Karthick, Sandesh, Subradeep, Satya, Saina, and Pratiksha. Karthick was from Kerala, a CA aspirant, and a solo traveler on this adventure. Sandesh was from Mumbai and worked for a power distribution firm. Subradeep and Satya were both from Kolkata and worked at an IT firm. Saina was also from Mumbai, and she was a badminton instructor as well as a national player. Pratiksha was also from Mumbai and worked for a sports brand. We were all from different sections of the country and worked in different fields.

Our driver now asked us to return to the bus because we had a long ride ahead of us. We still need to travel 150 kilometers to arrive at Sankri village before sunset. We returned to our seats, and the trip began. Saina and Pratiksha were seated in front of me, and we were debating the overall cost of our trip. They just told me how cheaply they booked this tour with Twist and Tour. It was quite cost effective. Meanwhile, I was gazing out my window at the breathtaking scenery of the Tehri Garhwal region near Nainbag. The views were breathtaking, with large mountains covered with greenery. You'll feel as if someone has just covered mountains in green bedsheets. I get a lot of satisfaction from looking at these mountain ranges. The terrible aspect of this journey was when Saina and Subradeep began vomiting.

For breakfast, our bus pulled over to a little dhaba. After seeing two individuals vomit, no one wanted to eat anything, but we would need a lot of energy because it was going to be a long day. Subradeep took a soda, while the majority of us had idli Sambhar with tomato catchup (I'm not sure why they gave catchup with it). Worst combination I could think of) Karthik and I ordered breadpakoda and chloe bathura. I had finished my breakfast quickly and was wandering around the little Dhaba. Many people on the bus, including myself, were experiencing motion sickness, and I didn't want to vomit. At the same time, I noticed a little medical pharmacy near the Dhaba. I went there and asked for motion sickness medicine; they gave me two for ten rupees. I bought a few candy and chewing gums to keep myself away from vomiting. I had to rapidly take one pill as a precaution.

With a few minutes remaining before our bus departed, Sarvanan and I decided to take a walk around around the area. We were both comparing these massive mountain ranges to the mountains of Ooty and Kodaikanal. We both agreed that the Ooty and Kodaikanal ranges are greener than here. Saravana was discussing how his wife encouraged him to go on this vacation. Family support is really vital while on this vacation. He also stated that he is pleased to work on a lower grade at the bank because it is easier to obtain leave and has fewer responsibilities, allowing him to travel more. It was now time to take a seat and board the bus.

While walking back to our seat, I noticed that our driver was not having his left ear. He was not deaf, but he had lost his left ear since birth. I told him how fortunate he is to drive on this path every day and view these lovely mountains. He responded that mountain ranges are magnificent, but driving the bus on this road is quite difficult because the route is in a mountain zone with a significant risk of landslides and bad weather. He also recalled an instance in which army personnel rescued him and other travelers during a landslide situation in which he was unable to proceed or return due to significant rains in the region, resulting in flood conditions. He had been trapped at a spot for more than 12 hours, which was extremely difficult for him because it was his obligation to securely transport all of the trekkers from Dehradun to Sankri. I became more concerned after hearing this conversation, and he was able to read my face. He just stated, "Don't worry, brother, the time has changed now." He smiled as he said, "The government has made good roads on this route, and there are many villages nearby; we will not face any such situation." I simply returned to my seat and prayed to all gods for a trouble-free trip. Our drive resumed, and I was feeling a little tired, but the scenery from the windows was keeping me awake.

Karthick vomited within the next 15 minutes, and Pratiksha was also experiencing motion sickness; I gave her the prescription, but it may have been too late because she began vomiting shortly after. I felt awful for Saina and Pratiksha when I saw Sandesh mocking them, but Karma is real. Sandesh vomited after another 20 minutes.

I've traveled a lot, but I've never seen so many people vomiting. It is fairly usual on this route, according to our driver. He suggested chewing candy and sucking on lemon. Everyone on the bus was fatigued and tired. Because there were few people sleeping, our driver opted to pull over near a river bank. It was the Yamuna river, which flows from the Yamnotri glacier at Bandarpunch. The river was looking lovely. The water was so pure that you could see rocks and sand in it. We went down to the river and shot some pictures. People were drinking this water, and our driver informed us that the water is used directly by the locals without any filtration. I also attempted to drink the water, but it was really freezing when I attempted to fill my bottle. It was 1:00 PM in the afternoon, and the water was ice cold. The river was full with water waves, and the water was moving at breakneck speed. There were large rock-like stones in the center of the river, and water flowed between them. We remained there for 15 minutes, taking in the landscape and listening to the river run. Everyone was revved up because the place was so dynamic. We decided to eat at the same location because there was a tiny Dhabha nearby. We all went there and placed our orders. I didn't want to eat a full dinner since I was frightened of vomiting, but I also didn't want to leave my stomach empty, so I ordered Maggie. Maggie was delicious. Later, I drank Pepsi and headed to the cash register. The owner of this Dhabha was quite nice, and the prices of all food items were very affordable.

Our driver called us at 1:30 p.m. and requested us to take a seat. He informed us that the next stop would be in 2-3 hours, so we should use the restroom before boarding the bus. We started heading towards Sankri immediately. As I returned to my seat, I attempted to call my mother, but there was no network coverage in that region. I went to sleep with the intention of calling her in an hour or two. I had been sleeping for about 30-45 minutes when I was startled awake by everyone saying "watch that", "take a picture", and I wondered what they were talking about.

We were now in the Uttarkashi Puraula area, and from here you can see snow-covered mountain ranges. The view was breathtaking; everyone was documenting it on their phones, while I was only catching it in my mind. It was the first time I saw so many mountain ranges covered with snow. The most challenging path was from Puraula to Sankri, which was full of zigzag roads. On one side, there are tall pines, and on the other, a large valley with views of a zigzag road and mountain peaks. During this route, the majority of those who had not vomited had vomited. Only I and the driver remained who had not vomited. I expected to vomit shortly, but our bus suddenly came to a halt, our driver used a hard brake, we wondered what had occurred, and then we noticed that he was vomiting. The one piece of advice I have for all of you who enjoy going in the mountains is to bring motion sickness medicine with you.

Later on, we arrived in a little village where a tourist bus had hit a car. We were trapped on a one lane road for 20 minutes because they were fighting. If this issue is not resolved, our driver told us that we would arrive in Sankri at night. The local person was furious because he had just purchased a new car, and the bus driver was trying to explain to him that the road was uneven, and as a result, he had hit his car, but the local guy was not willing to listen. Sarvanan noticed a nearby snack shop and went down to buy some snacks, while myself and Sandesh decided to go down and try to figure out this situation. We went to the local and asked him to let the bus driver park his vehicle so that we could take care of this problem as there is a lot of traffic behind the tour bus. He agreed, and traffic was cleared within a few minutes. Sarvanan brought breadpakoda for everyone, which was really hot and tasty. We were all relieved to be out of there because we were on our route to Sankri.

We were presently approaching Sankri village. We all felt cold, so we closed all the windows. We were all looking forward to this day. People travel from all over the country to reach the summit of the peak. Sankri is a fairly tiny town with only one lane of road access. There are a few vegetable and grocery stores, trekking equipment shop, one web café, a coffee shop, and a few lodges.

The Sankri Village in Uttarakhand is a route to The Paradise of Himalayas for every trekker. At Sankri, you will not only discover the lushness of The Himalayan Valleys of Uttarakhand but also get a chance to indulge in the local culture and have an insight in the lives of the Himalayan people. Sankri is the last village connected by bus. The village is about 13 Kms inside the Govind Wild Life Sanctuary (Netwair is the place where the check post is located).it is the roadhead to the almost untouched Har ki dun (3566m) with the Swargarohini Peak (6096m) towering above it in the backdrop.

You may now think how To Reach Sankri ?

There are various modes of transportation that are available to reach Dehradun

Direct Bus to Sankri: From Dehradun you can get direct buses to Sankri from Bus Station near Railway Station. The bus ply early morning from 7 AM to 8 AM and takes around 10 hours to reach Sankri.

Note: In case you missed early morning buses, then you can take Hanol bus which goes via Mussoorie and get down at Mori. From Mori you can take share or private taxis/bolero to reach Sankri. You can also take buses to Purola as well and then take taxi from there.

By Rail: The Dehradun Railway Station is well-connected with various major Indian cities like Delhi, Lucknow and Kolkata etc. The frequency of trains to Dehradun is quite high as it is the gateway to the Garhwal region of Uttarakhand.

If you have taken a package from a tour organizer then they will provide you pick-up and drop facility from Dehradun. I had taken a package from Himalayan Hikers.

Below is the list of 10 things which you can do in this village if you have time other than trekking or you are on a non-trekking holiday.

1) Old village temple

Plan your visit to the old temple having alluring wooden carvings and the architecture is worth to look at. Ask the priest and locals about the stories of "Devta" and all the mythological stories they have grown up hearing & believing them true.

2) Yoga for the soul

The outer temple premises have lot of space and mesmerizing views, you can plan a Yoga Session or even an exercise session there. Just imagine the views, surrounded by mountains, pure air and peace - the perfect place to get your body & soul fit.

3) Try the Herbal Tea

If you visit locals in the village, do ask them about the herbal tea they get from Jungles.It mainly keeps them warm from the cold climate. Even if you don't like to have Tea, I would suggest try this one, very nice in taste and different from the milk tea which is consumed in Indian households.

4) Village Walks

Take a walk around the village - markets , schools , playground, gardens, talk with the locals. Experience the slow paced village life of Sankri. Locals are very friendly and would be more than happy to tell you about their world and with all the curiosity would like to know about your world. How technology is bringing a change can also be witnessed.

5) Lunch at a Picnic Spot

Plan one of your lunches at the scenic spot of the village. You can have it at the summer house of a local or do a little hike of an hour or two & find your own spot or go down till the banks of Supin river or you can consider apple orchards that would be a beautiful place to have your lunch along with some juicy apples.

6) Cooking Class

Sign up for a cooking session to learn some unique recipes of Rajma and Apples. Lot of homes still have "Chulha" , you might get a chance to try your hands on the chulha and prepare some smoky food.

7) Try the Noodles & Momos in the Sankri Market

There is a shop run by Nepali Aunty in the Sankri market and she prepares yummy Noodles & Momos. Noodles are bit spicy but really delicious. If you find yourself wanting to eat something from the market, do try them, they open their shop around 5 P.M. in the evening.

8) Get yourself clicked wearing local dress

Get a picture or a selfie wearing beautiful locals dresses. The jackets & the local caps would make you look like one of them and it would be one of the unforgettable memories.

9) A day hike to Juda Ka Taal

I would recommend even a non- trekker to go out in the mountains and take a day hike to Juda Ka taal. It's basically a twin lake surrounded by grasslands which gets frozen in the winters. You can walk on the frozen lake in winters. And beautiful views are all around on the way to trek. This is the first campsite if you go to Kedarkantha trek.

10) Time for some souvenirs & shopping

You can buy local jackets , warm gloves, socks, sweaters woven by local women. These are available in the market and as well as in the local houses. You can check the Kurtis in the market, their designs are different and are quite cheap too. Lastly, do not forget to get some juicy & fresh apples.

It is a majestic place to experience the village life and hospitality of Himalayan locals.

We had arrived at our destination. Our tour leader greeted us. It had been a long road for all of us. Our guide assisted us in carrying our stuff and waiting in the common area. We were all fatigued and exhausted from the lengthy travel. We were waiting in the common area while they assigned us rooms. Karthick and I were assigned to the same room. We promptly got to our room, our hotel cum lodge was pretty spacious from the outside it did not appear to be so vast but they had more than 50 rooms, a common area, a dining area, a meeting place, and a little training facility. We were resting in our room when our guide knocked and informed us that we would be having evening refreshments and a briefing meeting in 5 minutes. We prepared for this and went to the dining space, with myself and Karthick being the first to arrive. The dining area is open, and you can see various mountain ranges from there. Meanwhile, our guide brought us tea, coffee, and Nutella sandwiches. We promptly grabbed it and waited for others to join us. Everyone arrived within the following 5 minutes, and our guide began briefing us.

Initially, he asked us to introduce ourselves and tell him if we had any prior trekking experience. Everyone began introducing themselves; interestingly, all of us had prior trekking experience. Our tour guide was delighted to hear that. He then began briefing us on our hike, informing us that it would be a four-day trek from Sankri. The first day we will stay at Juda Ka Talab, the second day at Kedarkantha Base Camp, the third day is our summit and we will stay in Hargaon, and the fourth day we will return to Sankri.

He says that the average nighttime temperature can reach -20 degrees Celsius. The whole trekking distance was 23 kilometers.He informed us that they would be taking our forest permit, as well as providing us with sleeping bags in tents, a medical kit, and an oxygen cylinder in case of an emergency. They will provide Crampons and Gaiters to every trekker.

Our guide informed us that there would be a total of two guides with our group. One will lead the group, while another will accompany the last trekker. If a trekker is unable to complete the trek due to a medical condition or other emergency, the last guide will accompany him back to camp. He also mentioned that there would be restrooms available during our hikes. It would be 200 meters from tents. If we need to use the restroom at night, we must go in pairs of two. Because it is a forest area and animals live there, you may spot one. If we spot an animal or a snake, our guide urged us not to yell, flee, or hurt them, but rather to simply move away and away from them. Generally, no animal will harm you unless they feel threatened.

He then described all of the equipment and personal apparel needed for the walk, such as:

1. Waterproof High Ankle Trekking Shoes
2. Waterproof trek trousers
3. Waterproof Jackets
4. Down Jackets (-10 to -15)
5. Trek Poles
6. Waterproof outer gloves
7. Fleece inner gloves
8. Headlamp / Torch
9. Neck warmer
10. Skull Cap
11. Sunglasses (Cat 3 or Cat 4 lens, anti UV, Polarized)
12. 2 pairs of thermals
13. 4 pairs of socks (2 cotton - 2 woolen)
14. T-Shirts (2 - 3)
15. Lightweight Trek Trousers or pants (2)
16. Inner wear

He advised us that if we did not have anything from the above list, we could buy or rent it from nearby stores. Fortunately, I had most of the items on the list on hand. He informed us that we must adhere to the times set for breakfast, lunch, and dinner. High tea will be served before breakfast and dinner. We will miss it if we do not adhere to the timetable provided by them. After the briefing, he informed us that our dinner will be ready by 9:00 p.m.

We all walked to a nearby shop to inquire about rent. I went to three separate establishments, all of which had the same rent prices. I was looking to hire a down jacket, trekking pole, and hand gloves. The total rent for all three was around 800 rupees. They demand your aadhar card or another form of identification, as well as a deposit of 1000 rupees. They will reimburse your deposit money and identity card once we have returned the gear to them at the end of the journey.

We decided to explore Sankri village after almost everyone leased a few pieces of equipment. There was a café near our hotel where I, Kartik, Pratiksha, Saina, Sandesh, Subdradeep, and Satya went for a cup of coffee. The café was nicely designed, but when we saw the menu and prices, we were shocked. We all decided to return to our rooms; however, on the way back, there was an internet café, and Satya needed to check a few emails from his clients. The cyber guy charged 100 rupees for 30 minutes of internet connection. While Satya was responding to his client's email, I realized that I had forgotten to notify my mother that I had arrived in Sankri. I was going to pay the cyber guy 100 rupees when the power went out. There was no network available in any of our cell phones. I arrived at my hotel, and happily, our hotel had an inverter, so I thought if they could give the wifi password, I could phone my mother. When I contacted my guide for a WIFI password, he informed us that the internet was not working due to a power outage in the entire area. I told him I needed to call my mother, and he generously gave his phone. I was surprised to find network in his phone; he was using a BSNL simcard having network. I instantly called my mother and informed her that I had arrived safely. I also told that this is my guide's mobile number, and you can reach me at this number.

It was about 9:00 p.m. when we all headed to the dining room. They had prepared delicious meals for us that included Punjabi Sabji, Roti, Rice, Daal, Salad, and Papad. They served us Gulab Jamun in the desert. We all had a good time at the dinner. After dinner, Karthick and I decided to go for a little walk. When we returned to our hotel, we noticed that everyone was sleeping in their rooms. We both went to our rooms to sleep.

This was our first day, and it was full of ups and downs. Overall, I had a good day because I wasn't vomiting and everything went according to plan. It was really cold in Sankri, so we were given two rough blankets. I had just gotten into bed and wrapped myself in blankets, and I can claim that I fell asleep within seconds in anticipation of exploring the next day.

CHAPTER FIVE

Juda Ka Talab: Mythical Ascent

Today, I woke up at 6:00 AM, and the first thing we did was divide our main luggage into a smaller backpack because we couldn't take all of it to the top. Following my guide's instructions, I only took a few essential items from my main luggage. I had a daypack bag in my luggage that could be easily separated, making it convenient for us to carry and walk. After about 20 minutes of sorting things out, I successfully packed my daypack bag and then got ready for breakfast.

We were supposed to have breakfast at 7:00 AM. Excited to start the day, Karthick and I went a bit early. Sarvanan and his friends were already there, and soon our guide arrived with high tea and breakfast. The rest of the team members also joined meanwhile, and we enjoyed our breakfast with a beautiful view of the mountain ranges.

While we were having breakfast, our guide started explaining the plan for the day. He said we would begin walking at 8:00 AM, and before that, we needed to check out from our rooms. He mentioned that he would conduct a final inspection of all the necessary equipment and clothing, and if anyone didn't have the required gear, they could rent it. During this inspection, they would also distribute crampons and gaiters to everyone.

After finishing our breakfast, we returned to our rooms, grabbed our luggage, and the organizer provided a specific room for us to keep our main luggage. Most of us stored our main luggage in that room, but Pratiksha and Satya decided to carry their whole rucksack with them during the trek.

After we finished all our preparations, we gathered on the main street where the owner of Himalayan Trekker joined us. He gave us some instructions about what to do and what not during the trek. Then, we all participated in a prayer for a safe summit. The prayer and ritual took about 5 minutes, and afterward, the owner distributed prasad to all of us.

While this was happening, there was a cute dog roaming around us. She was incredibly adorable, and if we gently tapped our hands on her head, she would shake her paw with us. We took pictures and videos with her. Normally, I am quite afraid of dogs, but she was different. She was very friendly with our whole group, effortlessly connecting with everyone she met. From the moment I saw her, it felt like we shared a delightful history of laughter and warmth. She wasn't just a cute dog; she was a heartwarming reminder that sometimes, the best connections are made with a wagging tail and a loving gaze.

Observing this dog, I genuinely believe they rank among the most joyful and loyal creatures on our planet. It's a universal truth that dogs don't demand anything material from humans; all they crave is our time and affection.

Inspired, I contemplated bringing a dog into my own home, but then I realized that if I couldn't dedicate ample time to a pet now, it wouldn't do justice to their companionship. Thus, I made a decision to welcome a furry friend into my life after retirement, envisioning it as a wonderful companion for the days to come. In a world filled with complex relationship dynamics and expectations, dogs stand out as beings that simply seek our attention and love.

We began the trek by invoking Lord Shiva, with Pratiksha and Karthick leading the way. Our destination for the day was Juda Ka Talab, and the trek was expected to take about 4-5 hours. After walking for around 15-20 minutes, we entered the Govind Wildlife Sanctuary. Initially, we were all dressed in three layers of clothes, but as we started climbing the mountains, it got warm quickly. Within the next 30 minutes, I, along with Sarvanan and his friends, took a 5-minute break. I was sweating a lot, so I decided to remove both my jackets and continued walking with just a single layer of fleece. Others in the group followed same.

When you start walking in the mountains during the daytime, your body generates heat. That's why you can just wear a fleece or T-shirt so that you won't sweat, and you can enjoy walking freely. After this short break, we resumed our walk.

After just 1 hour of walking, you begin to see snow around you. I started taking pictures of the snow and the mountain ranges. I've always loved mountains and nature since I was a kid. I had a dream of going on a trek, but I never mentioned it to my parents. During vacations, I usually went to South India or took classes like swimming and tally. Once I reached college, my focus shifted to setting up my future, and the dream of trekking was left behind.

With work commitments, taking a long break became challenging due to responsibilities. However, this time, I managed to take some time off to fulfill my childhood dream of going on a trek. Walking on the trail surrounded by snow felt like something out of a movie or documentary, and experiencing it in reality was a whole new adventure.

We took a break for some refreshments. I enjoyed the tea and Maggie. After resting for a few minutes, we started walking again because our guide said we need to reach our camp before afternoon. Satya and Pratiksha were carrying big rucksacks, and our guide took the rucksack from Pratiksha and carried it. Pratiksha and Karthick were leading the trek, and Sandesh was behind them. I was walking with Sarvanan, and behind me were Satya and Saina, with the rest of the trekkers following behind them.

During this trek, you'll never feel alone because there will be people from different groups either heading to Juda Ka Talab or returning to Sankri on the same route. We met trekkers who had already reached the summit and were heading back to Sankri. We asked them about their experience, and they described it as wonderful, fantastic, mind-blowing, and superb. One person even said it felt like being in heaven. After hearing their enthusiastic comments, we were even more excited to continue our journey. Along the way, you'll also encounter mules used to transport food, equipment, and tents. They have bells around their necks to signal their approach, and it's important to give them space as they walk.

A mule is a type of animal that comes from a mix between a donkey and a horse. It happens when a male donkey and a female horse have a baby together. People use mules because they are good at walking in snow, mud, and water. You often see mules in groups of 2 to 4, and there is a caretaker who takes care of them. The caretaker makes sure the mules don't block the trail for other trekkers.

Throughout the entire route, there is no network coverage. In some specific spots, you might get a signal for BSNL and Airtel, but it's limited. You can make regular calls, but the internet won't work.

I often ponder how life would be without the internet and network connections. Nowadays, we rely so much on our cell phones that we've almost forgotten the art of writing letters. While it's incredibly easy to make video calls or regular calls from anywhere in the world, it seems like we've forgotten how to truly live.

I've observed people visiting tourist spots, busy clicking pictures and shooting videos, but it feels like they're missing out on the present moment. They remember to capture memories in their electronic devices, but it seems they've forgotten to capture those moments in their hearts. Physically present at a beautiful place, but mentally preoccupied with work, business, exams, and the like – they worry more about their phone batteries than appreciating the beauty of the mountains. It's not that I'm against taking photos or videos; I just believe that at the same time, we should make an effort to soak in the scenery. Live in the moment, engage with your fellow travelers, make new friends, and relish the beauty around you. Enjoy the experience instead of just recording it.

As we trekkers strolled along, I often wondered about the purpose of it all. Why lug around this heavy backpack and put so much strain on our legs? The answer was surprisingly simple – we were gaining the opportunity to spend precious moments surrounded by nature. In that place, there was no air pollution, no honking traffic, and no one in a rush. It was just you and the serene embrace of nature.

The presence of towering pine and maple trees added to the beauty of the surroundings. Even if fatigue set in during the walk, witnessing the snow-covered peaks and enchanting trees provided a compelling reason to persevere and reach the summit.

Our trek guide was having a great time walking along the trail. He was jumping around, listening to local music on his Chinese phone. The music was loud, and even though we didn't understand the words, we enjoyed the beats.

The guide, an experienced mountaineer, told us stories as we walked. On the other side of the trail, there was a big mountain called the Black Peak of India. He proudly mentioned that he had climbed it three times. He was from Sankri village, and when we asked him about local life, he explained that kids have to travel at least 2 hours for higher secondary school. For college, they usually go to Mussoorie or Dehradun since there aren't many options nearby. It was surprising to hear that kids from Sankri village are studying despite the remote location.

Our guide had a special degree in mountaineering and loved hiking since he was a child. His passion for exploring the mountains was clear from his stories.

While we were walking, I spotted a tea shop that I remembered from a YouTube video. The unique thing about this tea shop is that the owner plays a beautiful flute once you place an order. I asked my guide if it was the same shop, and he confirmed it. Excitedly, we all decided to stop and enjoy some tea there.

What made this tea shop special was that it was surrounded by snow on both sides. To enter, we had to walk on a wooden platform because the snow had piled up everywhere. We ordered a glass of tea, and as we sipped it, the owner serenaded us with his flute. The way he played was incredible, and the sweet sound made me feel like sitting there and listening to it all day. It was truly an art.

Before leaving, we praised his skills, and he shared that many YouTubers who come to trek film him and make him viral, earning money in the process. Despite not getting any direct compensation, he expressed happiness in gaining more customers through the exposure.

We started walking towards Juda Ka Talab, where Pratiksha, Karthick, and our guide were waiting for all of us ahead to stay together. The place was beautiful, covered in snow. I had never walked on snow before. Right next to the path, there was some snow, so I tried walking on it. When I took my first step, I found out it was deep—about 3-4 feet. It's hard to tell how deep it is when you're close to it. The best way to check is to use your trekking pole by poking it before moving forward.

We all gathered there, and our guide told us it was time to wear crampons and gaiters on our shoes before going further. Putting on gaiters was quite easy, but getting crampons on our shoes was a bit tough. Luckily, our guide helped us. Crampons help you walk on snow by giving you a good grip, and gaiters keep your feet safe by stopping snow from getting into your shoes.

The Kedarkantha trek happens in winter, usually covered in snow from mid-December to mid-April. Snow starts right at the beginning, and after about 2 hours of walking, it's all snowy. It might seem easy in videos or pictures, but it's quite tough. Some say it's good for beginners, but that's not really true, especially if there's been recent snowfall.

The main motivation to keep going is seeing all the snow. The route looks beautiful with snow everywhere, like walking on a cold, white desert. Even though it might seem easy on YouTube, in reality, if there's been snowfall recently, it's pretty hard. The trail is narrow, with a big valley on the right and snow that could be really deep on the left—probably around 5+ feet. So, walking carefully on the trail is a must; going off the path isn't a good idea. If you're not used to walking much and are considering coming to this place, it's better not to attempt it. Make sure your body is in good shape before taking on this trek. While the trek is not that easy, the breathtaking views make it worth it. Don't hesitate; just pack your bags and go.

There are several myths with different versions of Kedarkantha and Juda-ka-Talab, a high-altitude lake located on the trail to the summit in Uttarakhand's Uttarkashi district. The stories revolve around Lord Shiva and what he did when he came to Kedarkantha.

According to the Kedarkantha legend, Lord Shiva sat at the summit to meditate but was disturbed by a bull, which was running below. So he went to Kedarnath, a town in Uttarakhand, to meditate afterwards.

Another local myth relates to the Pandavas, who went to the Himalayas to seek Lord Shiva's blessings. However, he hid from Bheem and disguised himself as a bull. But, Bheem recognised him and went after him. So Shiva hid underground. When he rushed out from his hiding place, he let his body parts get divided, and each part fell at a different place. His throat fell on the Kedarkantha, thus earning the peak its name- transliteration- "the throat of Lord Shiva".

The myth resembles the story of Panch Kedar, a set of five Shiva temples- Kedarnath, Tungnath, Rudranath, Madhyamaheshwar and Kalpeshwar- located in Uttarakhand's Garhwal region. According to this legend, the Pandavas, on the advice of Lord Krishna, sought Lord Shiva to pardon them for their sins of killing their kin during the Mahabharata war. But, Shiva was angry with them for their conduct and avoided them by taking the form of a bull and leaving for the Garhwal region.

The Pandavas sighted Shiva grazing as a bull in the hills of Guptakashi and tried to grab its tails and legs forcibly. However, the bull disappeared into the ground and later reappeared in the original form of Lord Shiva at five places- the bull's hump at Kedarnath, legs at Tungnath, face at Rudranath, stomach at Madhyamaheswar and hair at Kalpeshwar. It is believed that the Pandavas built five temples at these places.

Other major Himalayan peaks

During the trek to the Kedarkantha summit, the Swargarohini peaks (at an altitude of over 20,000 feet) will be clearly visible. They are Swargrohini 1, 2, 3 and 4. Swargarohini means a path to heaven. It is believed to be the way followed by the Pandavas, according to a local legend. However, only Yudhishthira out of the Pandavas is believed to have reached heaven. Another well-known mountain in this region is 'Black Peak' or Kalanag. The mountain resembles the hood of a black cobra and therefore derives its name from it. Near Black Peak lies another mountain called Bandarpoonch, which means monkey's tail and is named after Hanuman, the Monkey God.

Looking at these breathtaking mountain ranges, I couldn't help but feel a deep sense of gratitude. The sheer beauty of this place, tucked away in Uttarakhand, took me by surprise. We often get so caught up in our daily struggles, not realizing the hidden gems that exist in our own country. While we're familiar with the grandeur of the

Himalayan Ranges and the charm of Kashmir, the unique beauty of this location was a revelation to me.

As human beings, we tend to carry the weight of our problems, and if you ask someone about their issues, they'll likely have a couple to share. Life is full of challenges, but it's crucial to take a step back, unwind, and embrace a few days of relaxation each year. The uncertainties that follow events like COVID-19 remind us of the importance of turning our dreams into reality while we have the chance.

In my view, human life is an incredible gift bestowed upon us, and expressing gratitude for it should be a daily practice. Standing amidst these awe-inspiring mountains, my appreciation for the wonders of nature deepened, and I found myself feeling even more thankful for the experiences life has to offer. When the pressures of life become overwhelming, taking a break and going on a vacation can be a therapeutic remedy.

Reflecting on my own experiences, work had taken its toll during a demanding audit period. I remember feeling like a robot, working tirelessly. Late one evening, my mother, understanding the challenges I faced, inquired about my late return and prepared a warm meal for me. Despite the added responsibilities, I had made a conscious decision to take a break after the audit, and here I am now, surrounded by the tranquility of these mountains, turning that decision into a reality.

On my way to Juda Ka Talab, I saw a family heading in the opposite direction—from Juda Ka Talab towards Sankri. What caught my attention was that it was a family of three: a dad, a mom, and their son, who looked around 7 or 8 years old from his height. As they passed by, I asked if they had reached the summit. Surprisingly, they all had! I was amazed to hear that.

Out of curiosity, I asked the little boy if he ever felt tired from all the walking. With a smile, he said, "Yes, I get tired, but I love being in the mountains." Inspired by the kid's enthusiasm, I picked up my pace.

In trekking, there's a simple rule: take small steps when going uphill. It's like one step, one breath. Stay calm and avoid sitting down when you're tired. Just keep walking slowly, and you'll reach your destination. Many beginner trekkers make a common mistake during treks—they sit down whenever they feel tired, which actually makes it harder to walk. I recommend taking short breaks, maximum 15 minutes, and only after walking for at least 1 hour.

We had an additional companion in our group—an unexpected one. The dog we encountered outside the hotel was actually following us. I asked my guide if this was normal, and he explained that this dog routinely accompanies trekkers up to Juda Ka Talab every day. In the afternoon, the dog heads back to Sankri. The guide then shared a story about the dog and the Pandava.

First, let me tell you the story of dog that followed Pandavas.

After the great Mahabharat war, the Pandavas ruled the kingdom for 36 years. Then they decided to relinquish their kingdom and go on their last journey – Sanyasa and Vanaprastham. The five Pandava brothers – Yudhishtira, Bhima, Arjuna, Nakula and Sahadeva –and their wife Draupadi left for theHimalayas. They were followed by a Dog.

They started climbing the Himalayan mountains and soon one by one starting with Draupati, they fell down and fainted and died. Now only Yudhishtira, the eldest of

Pandavas, was left and keeping him company was the dog. Without looking back the two continued their journey.

Then one day suddenly Indra appeared before Yudhishtira in his chariot. Indra wanted to take Yudhishtira to heaven in the human form as he was the most pious among Pandavas and he was the one who had never strayed from the path of Dharma.

Yudhishtira refuses to enter the chariot without his brothers and Draupadi. Indra assures him that he will meet with them in heaven as they have already reached heaven.

Yudhishtira then asks the Dog to enter the chariot. But Indra objects to it. Indra states that we eat food by sitting on the floor and it is not possible to have a dog roaming in the same place. He also indicates that the presence of a dog will defile heaven. It is considered that a mere glance of a dog deprives the sacraments of their consecration.

But Yudhishtira is adamant; to him the dog appears as one who has been devoted, loyal in the time of loss of his brothers and Draupadi. He was faithful and loving in the hour of entire solitude. He cannot be happy in heaven as he would be haunted by the thought of the dog so true.

Finally, Yudhishtira decides to not to go with Indra and decides to stay with the Dog. The dog was not other than Yamadharma himself, Yudhishtira's father. He appeared before Yudhishtira and said, "You are indeed a great man, a righteous man; your compassion for all living beings is exemplary. A dog has been as dear to you as your own brothers. Your conduct will remain a shining example to all men for all times. Now, you can mount the chariot without any hesitation."

Yudhishtira was now satisfied; he bowed down to Yamadharma and Indra, and mounted the chariot. He reached Heaven with Indra. He was glad to find his kith and kin in Heaven. He felt happy to join them in divine life.

Our guide mentioned that, following that incident, there were noticeable genetic changes in dogs throughout the region. Whenever someone ascends to the summit, these dogs instinctively provide company to show the way, ensuring the trekkers don't feel alone. This tradition has been carried on since the time of Mahabharata and has become ingrained in the genes of these dogs. They are distinct from street dogs, exhibiting unique qualities.

He shared a few incidents where these dogs would bark if someone was about to step outside the trail, signaling a potential danger of falling into a deep valley. These dogs can also sense impending events like heavy snowfall or avalanches before they occur, leading to changes in their behavior. In such situations, they not only descend from the mountain themselves but also guide other trekkers to safety.

After hearing these remarkable stories, I became more certain that I would like to have a dog as a companion after my retirement.

Our guide let us know that we were just about 100 meters away from Juda Ka Talab. Along the trail, there were numerous other tents belonging to different trekking groups. One advantage of choosing Himalayan Hikers for our trek was that they had their tents strategically located with a view of Juda Ka Talab (Pond). Our guide mentioned that our trekking organization is the oldest and local, allowing them this unique advantage.

As we approached, we observed people from various camps enjoying themselves—singing songs, taking pictures, and creating reels. I couldn't help but think about how wonderful it would be to reach my tent and relax. Excitement filled the air as we hastened our pace to reach

Juda Ka Talab. In a matter of minutes, we arrived, and our tents were positioned just above the pond area.

Without wasting any time, I went straight to Juda Ka Talab. It was a captivating sight— the pond was blanketed with snow, and the water had turned into ice, resembling a giant ice cube. The initial plan of putting down my luggage and resting was quickly replaced by the sheer beauty of the frozen pond.

Juda ka Talab is a small high altitude lake between Sankri and Kedarkantha trek summit which is located at 9,100 ft above sea level. This lake is a mesmerizing site that offers scenic Himalayan landscapes. This is a beautiful camping spot for all the trekkers and usually a place to camp overnight. Out of all the existing charms of the Kedarkantha Peak Trek, Juda Lake is a place where you would be surrounded by thickets of tall trees and mountain slopes.

One local story of this lake is that Lord Shiva had come here to meditate. He wanted water, and he plucked a strand of hair from his bun (judaa) and threw it on the ground, which created the water body.

Locals also claim that long ago, there were two water bodies and they later connected (juda) to form the present one.

According to another story, a shepherd was herding his goats near the lake. He sat on a mound in the lake and played his flute, which fell into the water. He tried finding it but could not. Giving up, he took his goats and went to a village, where he had dinner in a woman's house. He found his flute on a table inside the house. When he asked her how she came by the flute, she explained that she was collecting water from a nearby stream and found it.

It is believed that there are several streams running from under the lake that move downstream. Hence, the name juda, meaning a connection between the lake and the streams.

This trek is surrounded by plenty of interesting myths and legends. You will also come across different versions of the stories I have narrated above.

I looked at the frozen lake with excitement, just like a kid looks at their favorite ice cream. Honestly, it seemed like a giant vanilla ice cream cup. It reminded me of a scene from a movie called "Charlie and the Chocolate Factory," where they showed a world full of chocolates. I couldn't help but imagine if this place could be like that - a huge vanilla ice cream or a big white chocolate pie.

I got lost in the beauty of the moment, standing there for almost 10 minutes. Little did I know, my guide was watching me. He finally said, "Vaibhav Ji, you can sit here for the whole evening, night, and tomorrow morning, but before that, let's have some food."

The trek was so amazing that I forgot I needed lunch. Honestly, I wasn't even hungry because the incredible views and experiences here were filling enough. My guide told me I'd be sharing my tent with Karthick, a relaxed and cool guy. Since we had shared a room the night before, I was happy with the tent arrangement. I quickly put my bag in the tent and went for lunch.

I walked to an open area where they were distributing our food. No one was around, and behind that space, there was a large tent. My guide invited me to see inside, and I found out it was the cooking tent. There was a cook and a helper preparing all our food, including roasted papad for everyone. Everything was ready—Roti, Sabji, Rice, Daal, Salad, and Papad. They started taking the food to the distribution area, and I helped them do so. Everyone was eagerly waiting to enjoy this lunch, and we all loved the delicious meal.

I couldn't help but feel for the cook and helper. They stayed in that tent, cooking for us in challenging conditions. They woke up early in the morning to prepare breakfast and slept late after finishing dinner. All of this was to ensure every trekker felt comfortable and got a homely meal.

After our lunch, our guide gave us some more instructions:

1. He showed us the toilet tent, which was about 100-150 meters away from our tent. Wet-toilets, the ones we use at our homes are not possible at camps. You need a proper drainage facility to let out all the wastewater. It will be a menace if people practise using these toilets at the campsites. You can very well imagine the situation very much similar to the ones in parts of cities where proper drainage is not available.So an alternative to wet-toilet is the dry-toilet. In these dry-toilets, a pit deep enough to accommodate waste and last for at least a week is dug. This pit has loose mud at your hands reach. And then to give this place a personal space, we cover this pit with a toilet tent. This type of toilet system to dump your waste is summed up as dry-toilet.
Once you are inside the toilet tent, you find a pit. This will be very much similar to the Indian-Style of Toilets. You need to squat down and find peace. After you are done, wipe yourself with a tissue paper. Dispose of the tissue itself along with the waste and then cover all the waste with the loose mud, already available at your hands reach. After covering up and leaving up no traces,

leave the tent all set for the next trekker.

2. The second instruction was clear: we were not allowed to enter the tents with our shoes on. Since our shoes had crampons, there was a risk of tearing the tent from the bottom. Our guide emphasized the importance of keeping our shoes outside the tent and strictly instructed us to follow this rule.

3. The third instruction was about avoiding walking on Juda Ka Talab today because, in the afternoon, the ice wouldn't be very strong. Our guide advised us to explore the frozen pond early in the morning the next day, before 7 AM. He explained that the night's minus-degree temperature would make the ice more solid, allowing safe walking. He cautioned that attempting to walk on the ice after 8 AM during the day could lead to breaking it, and anyone might fall into the extremely cold pond, making rescue challenging. He emphasized that even in the morning, before walking, we should use our trekking pole to check the ice's strength and then proceed cautiously.

4. The fourth and last instruction was that our high tea would be ready at 5:00 PM, and dinner would be served by 6:00 PM. Since we were in the mountains, the sunset occurred early. After sunset, our guide advised us not to wander far from the tent area. He demonstrated how to properly sleep in the sleeping bag, emphasizing that the nighttime temperature would be below freezing. Additionally, he informed us that if we needed to use the restroom, we should go in pairs for safety.

After receiving all these instructions, our guide mentioned that we were free to rest or explore nearby places. Sarvanan and his group opted to go into their tents and sleep. The rest of us decided to check out a nearby tea shop. When we got there, we discovered that they also offered campfires. Excitedly, we asked for a campfire for our group, but the charges were quite high due to the forest region regulations, and we couldn't afford it. Disappointed, we returned to our tents. Karthick and I were resting inside, and soon, Satya and Subradeep joined us because they were feeling bored. Later on, Sandesh also joined our group.

We started playing a game where we had to share the funniest incidents from our lives. Everyone took turns sharing their stories, and Satya had one of the funniest incidents. Unfortunately, I can't describe those stories here, but I can say that Satya had one of the coolest childhoods among us.

Eventually, they all returned to their tents, and Karthick and I continued to rest. I noticed that my mobile battery was very low, so I decided to use my power bank to charge it. Since there was no network in the area, I couldn't make any calls or send messages.

I took a short nap, maybe 15-20 minutes, and then woke up. I could hear people talking outside my tent, so I came out and joined in the conversation. It was time for our high tea, and as the sunset approached, we could all feel the cold setting in. Everyone headed to their tents to grab jackets from their backpacks, including me, as I could sense the chill in the air.

The weather here changes rapidly. I had seen on a YouTube video that mountain climates can change quickly, but I couldn't believe how fast it was happening. Even after wearing three layers of clothes (fleece, jacket, and down jacket), I still felt cold. We quickly had tea and decided to go for a walk to warm ourselves up. After a 150-meter walk, it started getting dark, so we decided to head back to avoid walking that distance in the night. Back near our tents, our guide noticed us all shivering from the cold. He reminded us that this was just the beginning, and we needed to do our best to stay warm.

Meanwhile, our dinner was ready and served. Surprisingly, everyone was eating quickly. We all wore gloves, and no one dared to take them off because it was so cold.

After we finished eating, we walked around the tents. Since it was dark, we had to use flashlights and headlamps. I used a flashlight my dad got as a gift from his client, and it worked really well, shining light far ahead. As it got colder, I noticed something interesting when Sandesh spoke—smoke-like stuff came out of his mouth. At first, I thought he might be smoking in the dark because I could see the smoke through his headlamp. Later on, I realized it was just condensation. That's when the cold air turns your breath into mist in winter.

As it got even colder, I looked up at the sky and was amazed. I'd never seen so many stars together, usually something you only see in movies. The stars looked really close, and they were beautiful. I told Satya, Sandesh, and Subradeep to look at the sky. "It's beautiful," Satya said. He wondered how we had missed it in the past 30 minutes.

The night view from Juda Ka Talab was unforgettable. Stars were everywhere, and we tried to take some photos. This was the best part of the day—looking at the stars from here.

It was almost 7:30 in the evening, and we were all feeling very cold. We decided to go to our tents and sleep. When I got back to my tent, I took off my shoes and entered. I realized I couldn't find my water bottle, so I turned on my phone's flashlight to locate it. After finding it, I took a sip of water and tried to figure out how to get into my sleeping bag. Unfortunately, my sleeping bag zipper was stuck, but thankfully, Karthick came to my rescue and helped me open it. Finally inside my sleeping bag, I closed my eyes and thanked God for showing me such a beautiful day with the snow, mountain views, and the stunning stars.

As I settled into my sleeping bag, I felt the intense cold around me. I placed my mobile and power bank in a pocket of my jacket to prevent the battery from draining. I was aware that the temperature would drop below freezing, and we had to endure the icy cold. Excited about the adventures awaiting us the next day, I closed my eyes, hoping to get some rest amid the freezing temperatures.

CHAPTER SIX

FOX ENCOUNTER: A NIGHT OF SILENT SHADOWS

I tried really hard to sleep because it was super cold, even with my cozy sleeping bag. But no matter what, sleep just wouldn't come easily. I closed my eyes, telling myself, "Come on, let's get some sleep." Managed to doze off for a bit, but I kept waking up. Every time I checked the time, it felt like it was barely moving. It was only 10:00 PM at one point, and Karthick was sound asleep. I gave sleep another shot and finally got some shut-eye.

I woke up again, checked the time, and it was 2:00 AM. I really needed to go to the bathroom and pee. I noticed Karthick was in a deep sleep, so I didn't want to disturb him while he was enjoying his sleep. I decided to get out of my tent. When I opened the zipper from the inside, I felt how cold it was outside. I thought it wasn't a good idea to wear shoes here and walk 150 meters to the restroom in the cold night.

I changed my plan. Our tents are more modern, and they can be opened from both the front and back. So, I thought I'd open the back side of my tent, walk on the ice for a bit, pee, and then quickly come back. I looked for my flashlight and found it under my sleeping bag. With the flashlight in hand, I was ready to go out.

I gently opened the back zipper of my tent and stepped outside. The first thing I did was close the zipper of the tent so that Karthick wouldn't feel the cold or get disturbed. I walked on the snow without shoes, just wearing a single layer of woolen socks. My feet could feel the cold. I turned on my flashlight and started moving forward. With every step, it felt like walking on small needles. I just wanted to pee quickly and come back, that was on my mind.

The snow from the night had turned into hard snow, and walking on it with just socks was a bad idea, I knew that. But going back to the tent to wear my shoes and then walking 150 meters to the restroom wasn't a good idea either. So, I decided to quickly walk ahead, pee, and go back without thinking too much. I was using my flashlight to see the ground, but then I realized I didn't need it.

I reached a point where I could see Juda Ka Talab shining brightly. I realized it was gleaming because of the moon's reflection. It was a full moon night, and the moon's brightness allowed me to see everything there.

It seemed like someone had placed big tube lights under Juda Ka Talab (Pond). Behind Juda Ka Talab, there were trees, and two dogs were playing there. The first thing that came to my mind was why these two dogs weren't sleeping and were playing in the snow. They didn't seem to feel the cold, but I knew their breed is different. They can easily survive in this kind of temperature.

I found a spot to pee. I put the torch in my mouth and started peeing. It felt so relaxing. On the right side, I saw Subradeep doing the same. He saw me and went back to his tent. Meanwhile, I heard the breathing of dogs near me. I turned my face back, and I couldn't breathe anymore. There was a family of red foxes. As I moved my face back, the torchlight was on the face of an adult fox, and he turned his face away because of the light.

The first thing that came to my mind was, if something happens to me, my mother will scold me a lot. I wasn't worried if they attacked me; I was more worried about my mother scolding me. I remembered what our guide told us. He said if any animal comes, don't shout, run, or react. Just calmly go away from them. I finished peeing and calmly walked back to my tent. I decided not to make eye contact with them, but at the same time, I was trying to see them because if they were going to attack me, I needed to run to save myself. I saw a baby fox with them in the group. The baby fox looked very cute. The baby fox saw that I was looking at him, and he then nodded his head towards the adult fox (maybe his mom or dad).

I walked really slowly so that the fox group wouldn't notice any sudden movement. I took tiny steps, and I could hear my heartbeat while walking. Finally, I reached near my tent. I quickly opened the tent zipper and went inside. Once inside, I wasn't sure what to do next. I wanted to inform everyone, but if I shouted, those foxes could attack us. When I saw the baby fox with the group, I realized that if I made noise, they might attack us to protect the baby fox. There were a total of 5 foxes, including the baby fox.

I unlocked my phone, thinking to call everyone, but then I remembered there's no network. Later, I decided to sleep, so I got into the sleeping bag and tried to sleep. I knew I wouldn't be able to sleep after the incident. I kept watching the time on my watch and thought of at least informing Karthick, but then I realized he's a young kid, and I didn't want to stress him out. I decided to let him sleep. It had been more than 45 minutes, and sleep eluded me. Suddenly, I thought about the foxes being outside the tents of Sandesh, Pratiksha, and Saina. If they went out for the toilet and saw the foxes, they might shout, and the foxes could attack them.

I was worried about their safety. I couldn't be a coward just sitting in the tent. I decided to go out, inform the guide about it. I quietly opened the tent and started putting on my shoes. I took my trekking pole and Karthick's trekking pole, thinking that if the foxes attacked, I could use both trekking poles to defend myself.

I slowly put one leg outside the tent while whispering the names of all the gods I could remember. I was heading towards the guide's tent, trying to walk quietly so that no one could hear me. The guide's tent was on the opposite side under a tree, and it was very dark there. I realized I needed a torch to go that far. Then, I remembered I accidentally left my torch outside the back of the tent when I entered.

I went back near my tent and quietly approached the backside from the right corner. Standing there, I tried to see if the foxes were around, but there was no one there. I went to the back of my tent and retrieved the torch. I looked around all the tents, and there were no foxes. I decided not to disturb anyone and thought it's better to go back to my tent and sleep.

I went back into the tent, got into my sleeping bag, and went to sleep. I stayed awake until 4:00 AM in the morning. It was hard to sleep after that incident, but eventually, I managed to fall asleep.

CHAPTER SEVEN

SUMMIT DREAMS AND SNOWMAN SMILES

I was in a deep sleep when I suddenly woke up to footsteps outside my tent. I noticed that Karthick wasn't next to me, and it was 6:20 AM. Despite not completing my sleep, I didn't feel tired. I left my tent and found Karthick and Satya already enjoying morning tea. I joined them and had a glass of tea. Our guide were getting ready for the journey to the base camp, so I approached him and discussed the fox incident. I wasn't sure if it really happened or if it was just my imagination due to the extreme cold.

He asked where I saw them, and I mentioned it was just behind Sandesh's group tents. We went there, and there were footprints. After seeing them, the guide confirmed that I had indeed seen a group of foxes the previous night. He explained that it's rare to spot them in this area, and they usually don't come close to humans. They might have come in search of water. He advised me not to share this incident with other trekkers as it could scare them. We both agreed to keep it to ourselves.

While talking about the incident, my guide shared a similar trekking experience he had in Himachal Pradesh where he encountered a snow leopard. Snow leopards are very rare to see, with only about 500 in India, usually found in high-altitude areas. He recounted leading a trek when a snow leopard appeared in front of them. He admitted feeling scared and unsure of what to do next.

He decided to quietly step back and prevent the other trekkers from advancing. After waiting for about 30 minutes, they returned to the same spot, and the snow leopard was gone. He emphasized the importance of not reacting in front of these animals and suggested quietly changing your route as the best solution.

In the midst of our conversation, he used a walkie-talkie to contact the Sankri Base Camp. He informed them about the incident so that they could alert the forest guard. This way, the forest guard could caution other trekking guides and companies to take necessary precautions.

I felt scared and worried after the incident, and it was evident from my expression. My guide comforted me with two important points:

1. "Vaibhav ji, we have entered their homes, not them."

2. "If we don't react, they won't react. Most animals only attack humans when they feel threatened or in self-defense."

Reflecting on a previous visit to the famous Gir Sanctuary in Gujarat, known for its Asiatic lions, I recalled taking a jungle safari there. Our guide emphasized a similar point that animals typically don't attack humans without a reason. It could be due to feeling unsafe, self-defense, or a loss, like a missing or deceased child.

This incident became one of the most challenging moments in my life. In such situations, there are moments when you may not know what to do next. However, it's crucial not to lose our senses during such moments.

I noticed Sandesh and Satya heading towards Juda Ka Talab. Without wasting any time, I hurried to join them because I wanted to walk on it too. Taking the lead, I checked the solidity of the frozen lake using my trekking pole—it was rock solid. After me, Karthick and Satya followed. The three of us were now walking on the frozen lake of Juda Ka Talab. Describing this experience in words wouldn't do it justice; it was truly mind-blowing. We reached the center of the lake, capturing photos and videos. With each step, we made sure the ice was strong before proceeding, taking precautions.

Meanwhile, our guide called us for breakfast, and we all headed back. Today's breakfast was South Indian upma with toasted bread butter. We relished the delicious food, and soon, the others joined us.

After enjoying our breakfast, we went back to our tents, grabbed our backpacks, and got ready for today's journey. Since everyone else wasn't ready yet, Karthick, Satya, and I went to Juda Ka Talab and sat on big rocks near it. We started singing songs one by one, and Satya's voice was really good. We enjoyed the moment, sitting by the frozen lake, singing our favorite songs, and appreciating the beauty of nature.

In that moment, I realized how busy we are in our city lives, trapped in concrete jungles. We often forget to explore beautiful places that might be quite close to our homes. It's not necessary to travel far every time; you can visit nearby mountains, beaches, lakes, rivers, and forests for a day trip. Even a simple visit to a garden can turn into a great evening, bringing positive vibes without the need for extensive travel.

These days, people prefer not to wake up early in the morning for trips. They seek entertainment in activities like going to expensive resorts, amusement parks, and theaters, not realizing they could have more fun exploring natural places.

We all crave comfort when it comes to travel. I understand that time constraints affect everyone, but taking one or two extra days off won't halt the world. Many of us live in big cities, surrounded by towering buildings or bungalows. Yet, how many of us witness the daily sunrise or sunset?

The answer is simple. We are all caught up in the rat race for money. While I acknowledge that money is crucial for survival, living your life is equally important. It's about living the life you want. If you enjoy boating, do it; if you like trekking, go for it; if you have a passion for swimming, dive in. Don't wait for the perfect time because there is no such thing. You have the power to make the time right with your own willingness.

I saw everyone with their backpacks, our guides were ready, and so were we. We started from JUDA ka Talab to Kedarkantha Base Camp. Karthick, Sarvanan, and I took the lead this time. We began walking uphill. My advice to everyone is to avoid carrying too much luggage. If budget allows, consider giving your luggage to porters. It will make walking easier for you.

As we moved forward, we reached a high point where we could see JUDA-Ka-Talab, and it looked amazing. The lake appears different from every angle, and from here, it resembled frozen white lava flowing from a volcano. The trees around the lake added to its beauty. This spot offered a special view because not only could we see the lake, but also the mountain ranges behind it. The beautiful views brought smiles to our faces as we continued towards the base camp.

The initial path from here seems easy, with white snow on both sides of our trail. Let me make it clear that, despite what you might see in videos or read, this trek is not easy. Karthick was enjoying the journey, and his enthusiasm motivated all of us. Gradually, we started enjoying our little steps one by one. Even though it was 10:00 AM, we didn't feel the sun, as we were walking under a dense forest covered in snow. On the left side of our trail, we could see the beautiful Himalayan ranges. Most of the peaks were covered with snow, resembling a chocolate ice cream with a topping of vanilla. We all cherished this special view.

Today, we need to be extra careful while walking because on the right side of our trail, there's a valley. If we place our feet too much to the right, there's a chance we might fall into the valley. The valley isn't very deep from here, but it's covered in snow, and getting yourself out could be tough. Be extremely cautious at this part of the walk. Don't rush; take your time, enjoy the view, chat with others, and walk slowly. The distance we're covering today isn't too long, so it's better to savor the scenery and proceed without hurrying.

As we continued on the trail, we came across something amazing. There was a huge tree that had fallen onto the path. The tree was so big that we could easily walk beneath it. Layers of snow covered it, resembling toothpaste on a brush. We all passed under the tree, enjoying the experience. I couldn't help but wonder how the local people manage to survive in this kind of weather.

The views today are exceptionally special because there is snow as far as your eyes can see. Moreover, we felt quite comfortable walking today, perhaps because our trek yesterday warmed up our legs. Saina and Subradeep were right behind me; Subradeep, who was exhausted yesterday, walked comfortably today because before the start of our journey today, he gave his luggage to a porter. All of us were doing our best to enjoy the views at every point along the way.

Taking small steps from Juda ka Talab, we didn't realize we had reached Kedarkantha Base Camp. I checked the time, and surprisingly, it took us only 45 minutes to get there. The base camp is beautiful, offering panoramic views of snow-covered peaks like Bandarpoonch, Swargarohini, Kala Nag, and Ranglana. The Kedarkantha peak is clearly visible too.

When we reached the tent area, our guide told us they couldn't assign us a tent right away. Another team that went for the summit today hasn't returned, and their belongings are still in the tents.

We put our backpacks in the common area of our tent. Everyone began taking pictures and videos. I wanted a video of myself falling in the snow, so I asked Karthick to record it. He started recording, and I opened my arms, falling onto the snow. The snow here was different; it wasn't soft but hard. Believe me, as soon as I fell, my back started hurting. Thankfully, I didn't fall from a great height; otherwise, it could have been a serious injury. So, to all my readers, a message: before playing in the snow, make sure to check if it's hard or soft snow.

We were having a good time, and I went back to where our backpacks were kept under a plastic sheet. I noticed there was enough space on the plastic, so I decided to lie down and take a nap. I used my backpack as a pillow, placed my head on it, and put on my sunglasses. Closing my eyes, I started resting. Everyone else saw what I was doing and decided to join in. The problem was that we didn't have enough space for everyone, but somehow, we managed to make it work.

Meanwhile, the trekkers who went for the summit today returned to the base camp, retrieving their belongings from the tents. We asked them about the view and whether it was an easy trek. They shared that the sunrise from the peak was beautiful. As they started heading down towards Hargaon, our guide replaced the sleeping bags with fresh ones. Karthick and I placed our bags in the tent.

Our neighbors were Satya and Subradeep. While we were in our tents, the guide announced that lunch was ready. We all came out and began having our meal. Today, the cook prepared Punjabi Sabji, Roti, Chawal, and Daal. The food was excellent, and we all enjoyed it. After eating, we went for a short walk, visiting a tea stall about 150 meters uphill from our tents. On the way up, we passed many other tents.

The tea shop had a great location. From there, we could see the entire base camp with numerous tents and people. Our tents looked tiny from this vantage point, resembling colorful cherries in yellow, orange, and green. I asked the owner how much a glass of tea cost, and he said it was 50, so I asked for one. While he prepared the tea, I inquired about how he stayed in this place. He explained that he did stay here; instead, in the evening, he goes to Hargoan where he has accommodation and stays there. The shopkeeper also had kids with him, and they stayed together. I asked if the kids went to school, and he replied affirmatively, mentioning that they attended school in Sankri village and during holidays they come to help him.

The shop owner traveled to Hargoan daily to bring milk, vegetables, and other groceries to Kedarkantha Base Camp. He carried everything by himself. When I questioned why he didn't hire a mule or porter, he explained that doing so would increase the cost of his products, making it unaffordable for many trekkers. Instead, every morning, he informed his wife about the groceries he needed, and she brought them from Sankri to Hargoan. The next morning, he transported everything to the base camp.

During this conversation, my tea was ready. I tasted it, and without a doubt, it was the best tea on the trek—absolutely awesome.

I sipped my tea, enjoying the stunning view of the Himalayan ranges and pondering a simple thought: why hadn't I come to such places or tried trekking before? It has been one of the best experiences in my life, no doubt. Despite the cold, the views here have a way of warming you. I couldn't help but think that if I could show this place to my parents, they would be so happy. Of course, it would be quite a challenge for them to walk and stay in this atmosphere.

After finishing my tea, I noticed an elderly man entering the tea shop and ordering tea without sugar. We exchanged smiles, and I couldn't resist asking him his age. He said he was 82 and on a solo trip. I thought this person might be an interesting guy, so I decided to sit and talk with him.

I asked him first why he was doing a solo trip at his age. He explained that he was from Bangalore and had worked in a private company for 35 years. After retiring, he took on the responsibility of caring for his wife and grandson since his son and daughter-in-law were both working professionals. Unfortunately, his wife passed away last year, and now that his grandson has grown up, he decided to fulfill his long-held dream of traveling and exploring the world.

He shared that during his working years, he couldn't go trekking because he needed to save money for his son's education. Additionally, his wife, a very religious lady, would often compare his travel plans with temple visits. Despite wanting to explore, he prioritized his family's needs.

The uncle mentioned that his wife, though not highly educated and content with simple things, never asked for anything. She would wear old or even torn sarees without making demands. Her only request was to take her to temples. The uncle explained that this was a significant reason he never said no to her. He kept his own wishes in his heart because sometimes, what matters more is the happiness of others over our own desires.

After retiring, the uncle took on the additional responsibility of caring for his grandson as his wife was unwell and always on medication. Trekking was not on his mind during that time. However, after his wife passed away last year, he thought about trekking again, especially now that his grandson was grown up. But before he could decide anything, he faced serious medical issues.

The uncle shared that he had undergone two bypass surgeries and had a pacemaker implanted in his heart, all within the past year. I was unsure how to react. He continued, saying that when he informed the doctor about his plan to go on this trek 20 days ago, the doctor said it was like committing suicide. The uncle responded that even if he didn't live much longer, attempting this trek or dying during the journey would be without regret, as he tried to fulfill his dream.

I asked how his son allowed him to come here, and he explained that his son hadn't allowed it, but his grandson convinced him. The grandson had a strong attachment to him, managing all the bookings. Although the grandson wanted to come along, the uncle preferred doing the trek solo. His grandson arranged a special guide and porter for him to ensure his comfort.

I was surprised to hear all this. We often hear that there's an age for everything, but in reality, if you have the will to do something, age is not a factor. This uncle motivated me a lot.

Before leaving the tea shop, I asked the uncle what he hoped to achieve by doing this. He said it was about fulfilling his dream and challenging himself mentally. He emphasized that he wasn't doing it to prove anything to the world but to prove to himself that, yes, he could do it.

I left the tea shop but couldn't shake off the thoughts from the conversation I had. Sometimes, we get so caught up in family, work, or business responsibilities that we forget to make time for ourselves. We should all pursue what we want in life. It's not about how long we live but what matters the most is how much life we truly experience, fulfilling all our dreams into reality. Eating what you desire, doing what you want, and traveling wherever you wish—that's the true meaning of living life on your terms.

I noticed Satya, Karthick, Subdradeep, and Sandhesh working on something near the tea shop. I joined them and saw they were attempting to make a snowman. The snow here wasn't too hard, making it easy to shape. Initially, the bottom layer of the snowman resembled a Shivling. Sandesh went a bit further to find softer snow, rolled it up, and created the upper layer. After about 40 minutes, we had a snowman, but it lacked eyes and hands.

Spotting a tree near the tea shop, I gathered a few branches lying on the ground and brought them to the snowman. We divided two branches equally and fashioned hands for our snowman.

Now, we needed something for eyes. I had an idea and went back to the tea shop, where I had seen many empty plastic bottles. I removed the caps from the bottles and brought them to the snowman. Satya fixed these caps as eyes for our snowman.

Sandesh found a muffler near the trail, adding it around the snowman's neck. Our snowman looked fantastic, and people from nearby tents came over to take pictures with him. It was great teamwork. The only thing missing was the nose. As we were coming down, I spotted a pen cap on the trail. I quickly grabbed it and placed it as the nose for our snowman.

With blue eyes made of bottle caps, a red pen cap nose, brown hands from tree branches, and a black muffler around his neck, our snowman looked like a true gentleman.

We reached our tent area, where everyone was outside taking pictures. Just above our tent area, there were other tents. We noticed a girl in a saree wearing high-heeled sandals, walking on the snow while her friends recorded a video of her. The younger generation can go to great lengths for views, I thought. Our group watched her from a distance and laughed at what seemed like a silly stunt. The temperature at that time was around 2-3 degrees, and wearing a saree and dancing in high heels was not a good idea. She fell three times while making the videos, which could have been really dangerous if she got injured.

I'm not against making reels or TikToks, but at least be safe while doing it. Sandesh called me over, and we started taking pictures from our spot. The sunset was about to happen. Sandesh, Satya, and Subradeep suggested some poses, and I followed their suggestions while they took pictures.

We also posed in the famous style of Akshay Kumar from the movie "Phir Hera Pheri." Pratiksha and Saina must have taken 100-150 pictures during that time. I noticed that the sunset was occurring, and I wanted to capture it. The sunset was beautiful, happening behind the ranges of Ranglana, Kala Nag, and Swargarohini. It was so memorable. Watching that sunset felt like it was taking away all my bad memories and negativity.

There was another group ahead of our tents, all from Mumbai. Sandesh and I went near them because the sunset view from that spot was very nice.The group indulged in alcohol and smoking at the location. Consuming alcohol at high altitudes is not recommended. Many people treat this place as a picnic spot without realizing the risks involved. I've come across numerous videos where individuals consume alcohol at high altitudes without understanding the potential dangers. Furthermore, because of reduced air pressure at higher elevations, alcohol enters the bloodstream more rapidly and has a prolonged effect on the body. This heightened risk can result in dehydration, nausea, vomiting, headaches, and lightheadedness.

It wasn't just the Mumbai group that was smoking there; I observed many others indulging in smoking at tea shops, outside their tents, or along the trail. The issue lies in the fact that they don't comprehend the prohibition of smoking in public spaces. India was the first country globally to enact a law prohibiting smoking in public areas, though enforcement remains lax. Nonetheless, people should exercise maturity and refrain from smoking openly.

The beauty of this place is marred by those who bring alcohol and cigarettes. This isn't the appropriate setting for such activities. If one wishes to smoke or consume alcohol, it's advisable to do so in designated areas like pubs or at home, not in the mountains. Some individuals believe they appear cool and sophisticated by engaging in such behaviors, but in reality, they are compromising their own health.

Sandesh mentioned that there was network available there, so I asked if I could use his mobile to call home. He handed me the phone.

I quickly called my mom, and as soon as she heard my voice, she asked only one thing: "Have you reached the top?" I informed her that we would be reaching the top tomorrow, and our guide told us that most cellular networks are available on the peak, so please be online between 06-08 AM tomorrow. She wished me good luck for the next day, and I returned the phone to Sandesh.

Meanwhile, our guide called us for high tea as the sun was setting and we could feel the increasing cold. Before enjoying high tea, we all went to our tents to grab our jackets. I went to my tent and put on both jackets. Finally, we gathered for high tea, and the guide informed us that lunch would be served within the next 20 minutes. After that, we needed to go to our tents and rest.

It was crucial for all of us to sleep before 07:00 PM because the next day we had to wake up at 02:30 AM, have breakfast, and start walking towards the final summit by 03:00 AM. Tomorrow would be a day of extensive walking, requiring a lot of energy. So, the guide clearly instructed us to be in bed by 07:00 PM.

In the chilly weather, we quickly had our tea and headed to our tents. After 20 minutes, our guide called us for dinner. Personally, I decided to skip it as I wasn't hungry and needed some rest. Karthick and I stayed in the tent.

Attempting to sleep in such an atmosphere was challenging. Although we managed to sleep, it wasn't as deep as we had hoped. Around 10:00 PM, I felt something falling on our tent or a strong wind. It was so cold outside that I didn't want to open the tent and check. I asked Karthick if he felt the same, and he thought it was just the wind due to our tents being in an open area at a high altitude. I set an alarm for 02:25 AM and tried to sleep.

Sleeping in the tents on the snow, inside sleeping bags, was uneven, but we somehow managed to get some rest. We were excited about the next day, anticipating it to be very special as it was the final summit day. We knew it would be challenging, and at the same time, we needed to conserve energy and rest.

Lost in these thoughts and excitement, I eventually fell into a deep sleep.

CHAPTER EIGHT

WHISPERS OF KEDARKANTHA: A NEW BEGINNING

At 1:00 AM, I woke up because I thought something on the edge of the tent had fallen. When I tried to touch it from inside the tent, I couldn't feel anything. I decided to go back to sleep and was dozing off. Around 2:00 AM, our guide started shouting and told us to shake our tents. He explained that there had been heavy snowfall since 10:00 PM the previous night, and snow was accumulating on the tent roofs. He instructed us to shake our tents to make the snow fall off.

Then, he gave us the most disappointing news that the summit would not be possible that day and asked everyone to stay in their tents. It was a heartbreak for all of us. We had come for the summit, and now, because of the snowfall, we couldn't make it to the peak.

It was dark and cold outside. Our guides told us to stay in our respective tents until their next call. Every half hour, our guide came near our tents, asking us to shake them to let the snow slide off. We continued this exercise until 6:00 AM in the morning.

At 6:00 AM, he allowed us to come out. We unzipped our tent, which had two layers of zips. We had placed our shoes between these layers to prevent them from getting cold. When we opened the first layer of the zip, about 2-3 kg of snow entered our tent. Our first task was to throw the snow out, which took us 10 minutes. After clearing the snow, we started searching for our shoes, and we found them completely covered in snow, with snow inside the shoes as well. It took us another 5 minutes to remove the snow from both shoes. Finally, we wore our shoes and stepped out of our tents.

Snow covered everything. The trails near our tents vanished beneath a blanket of snow. Looking at our tents, I noticed they were buried under at least 2-2.5 feet of snow. Our guide worked tirelessly to clear the snow from outside the tents, ensuring our safety. Layers of snow covered all the tents, tables, chairs, and every surface around.

This was my first time witnessing snowfall. I initially thought it might feel similar to rain, but it's quite different. Snowfall is unique; it's very gentle, like tiny balls descending on you. Intrigued, I removed both layers of gloves to truly experience it.

I extended my palm a bit away from my body, allowing the snowfall to land on it. Surprisingly, I couldn't feel anything on my palm; there were small snowballs resting on it. Using my other hand, I gently touched the snowball, and it instantly broke apart. The snow was incredibly soft, now resembling white powder.

This encounter with snowfall was truly a priceless moment for me.

My guide noticed me enjoying the moment, and suddenly, he threw a ball of snow at me, welcoming me to the Himalayan Mountains. I smiled and quickly made a snowball to welcome him back. Sandesh was already outside, and he joined in the fun.

Our laughter and playfulness attracted the attention of the rest of our trekking group, and they all came out to join the snowy excitement. I started capturing videos and photos because it was my first time experiencing live snowfall, and it was truly amazing.

This snowfall was a unique and special experience for all of us. It was the first time we were witnessing it in person. We played in the snow, threw snowballs at each other, made videos, and took photos. For those moments, we almost forgot that we had missed our summit for the day.

Meanwhile, our guide called all of us because they had prepared high tea for us. They wanted to place the tea and coffee kettle on the plastic table, but the table was completely covered with a layer of snow. With the help of our trekking poles and our hands, we removed the snow. Our guide placed the kettle, and we all started having tea one by one. The tea was very hot, but we couldn't feel the warmth because it was too cold at that time. Even the hot tea didn't feel hot in that chilly weather.

Our guide informed us that since last night, continuous snowfall had covered all the trails toward the summit with snow. Now, it will take at least 3-5 days to create a new trail. The snowfall had not stopped; it was still falling. We were all sad that the summit was not possible today.

I was in deep shock, and so was everybody else. Pratiksha, Karthick, and I did not want to give up so easily. We requested the guide to allow us to make an attempt to climb the peak. Our guide just asked us to go to the tea shop, which was 100-150 meters away, and come back. The three of us started going there.

We started walking in the snow. Our legs were almost 1 foot under the snow. It was very difficult to find the trail. But since we had gone there the previous day, we got some idea of the trail, and we were walking accordingly. We all took each step carefully, one step at a time, with the help of our trekking pole.

Somehow, we reached there and realized that it would not be easy for everyone to go to the peak. Snow was everywhere. There were a few other trekking groups there who were requesting their guide to take them to the peak. They were ready to take the risk, and the guide also agreed. We all came back to our tents.

Our guide could read our faces. He came to ask and said, "Can anyone see the peak of Kedarkantha?" We all said no, we couldn't see anything. Due to the heavy snowfall and bad weather, the visibility had decreased a lot. The sky was still not clear. We informed the guide that one group is attempting to go up on the peak, can we join them?

He clearly said no and told us that we were his responsibility. He added that no one can go to the peak today. He made us understand that without a clear vision, we would not know the direction of the trail. If those people are going, they could go a maximum of 500-600 meters, not more than that.

Certainly, all three of us realized that summiting is not possible today. The dream of climbing the peak would still be a dream for all of us. There was sadness in our eyes and pain in our hearts for not being able to reach the top. All of us came here to go to the top, but today we are not able to do the same.

I was very upset at that moment. It felt like I was so close to this peak, and I am not able to summit it. Certainly, my mind gave a thought that yes, Vaibhav, today you have not climbed the peak, but at the same time, you have witnessed the snowfall that is happening. There are always some gains in failures. Today's gain for all of us was watching the snowfall live and coming till the base camp itself, like climbing the peak. This trek was a test for me, whether I would be able to do it or not, and certainly, I made it to the base camp. I was successful in this examination. I did not give up; I enjoyed the snowfall.

I made up my mind that I should not have any regrets about not reaching the peak. Meanwhile, our guide called us all and gave us a choice. The first choice was that we can stay today at Hargoan, and then tomorrow we can go to Sankri as per the old schedule. The second choice was that today itself, we will go back to Sankri, and tomorrow we can go to Dehradun. We all selected the second option because this second option will give us one more day. With this one more day, we can explore Dehradun, Mussoorie, Haridwar, or Rishikesh.

We all decided to go back to Sankri today itself. We went back to our tents, picked up our backpacks, and got ready. Before the final goodbye to Kedarkantha Base Camp, we had a group picture. We all started going down. While going down, I realized that this snowfall had not stopped yet. There were huge trees around us, and their leaves and branches were covered in snow. It looked so beautiful. I felt like it was the month of December, and Santa Claus would be coming soon to give gifts to us. The scene from here was so promising.

I saw a bird sitting on a branch of a tree. The bird looked like it had extra hair on its body, appearing fat around the belly. I showed the bird to our guide, and he informed us that this bird is called the Himalayan Snowcock. We all watched the bird. From below, we thought the bird was sitting alone, but when she opened her wings, we saw two small Himalayan Snowcock baby birds underneath. The babies were watching the snowfall, and snow landed on the mouth/nose of one baby bird. It shook its head and removed it. This scene looked so beautiful.

One more advantage of reaching the Kedarkantha summit was that we could slide down on the snow while returning to the Base Camp. Our guide had an alternative plan, and there were a few places on the way back to Sankri where we could still enjoy sliding. So, at a particular point, he asked us to stop and take turns sliding down. It turned out to be a fantastic and fun activity for the day. We all slid down on the snow, reliving our childhood and thoroughly enjoying this playful part of the journey.

After our first sliding experience, everyone wanted to continue descending by sliding. Our guide pointed out the way, indicating where it was possible to slide down until Juda Ka Talab. The frozen lake, Juda Ka Talab, was entirely covered in snow, and the tents where we had stayed two nights before were buried under a thick layer of snow. Only the top parts of the tents were visible.

The snowfall had stopped, and now the clear sun was visible in the sky. As we descended, we found opportunities to slide, making our journey down faster and more enjoyable. We slid almost halfway, avoiding the need for extensive walking.

After reading this, I'm sure you'll be eager to see some photos from this journey. I've created an Instagram account where I've posted all the pictures and videos. You can find them on the Instagram page named "Kedarkantha

Whispers." Additionally, a short video of this journey is available on my YouTube channel, "Being HR."

Feeling hungry, we decided to take a short break near a tea shop. I ordered a delicious Maggie for myself. After a 20-minute break, we resumed our journey towards Sankri.

We were just an hour away from Sankri when the challenge began. Three days ago, there was hard snow in this area, and now it was melting. The melting snow had created waterlogged soil, turning the path into mud. It became tricky, with everyone slipping and sliding. Satya, in particular, struggled to maintain balance and ended up breaking his trekking pole. Descending became a cautious process for all of us.

After 20 minutes on this challenging route, we took a break. Our shoes were now coated in mud, and trek pants were smeared everywhere. My shoes had crampons, and I attempted to remove them, but mud made it challenging. I gave up. Observing my struggle, my guide came to the rescue. He used my trekking pole, wedging it between the crampon and the edge of the shoe. In just a second, my crampons were removed. It brought relief as walking with crampons in muddy conditions was proving to be quite difficult for me.

I took a break, removed my leg from the shoe, and rested for about 15 minutes. After this short break, I resumed my descent. The path remained muddy throughout, and I proceeded cautiously, carefully checking each step. Coming down requires careful attention because most accidents occur during the descent, not during the ascent or summit climb. The excitement to return quickly often leads to accidents. I had witnessed numerous people falling on the trail while descending, so I proceeded with caution, avoiding unnecessary risks. My guides were supportive and took good care of me during the descent.

I had descended and reached the road, but the trail was very muddy, causing me to fall several times on the way back to Sankri. Despite the slippery path, I was relieved to have returned safely without any injuries. It took an additional 15 minutes to reach our hotel from there. By the time I reached the hotel, it was 02:30 PM. Fortunately, there was electricity, so I requested the wifi password from my guide. After connecting to the internet, I was surprised to find numerous messages on WhatsApp from various groups. For almost 10 minutes, messages kept pouring in. Later, I called my mother via WhatsApp and shared the day's events with her. While she tried to offer words of encouragement, there was a hint of sadness in her voice. She asked me to share all the pictures, and I promptly did so.

I collected my bag from the common area and headed to the room assigned to Karthick and me. Karthick was already there, waiting. After a refreshing shower and a change of clothes, I, feeling exhausted from the day, decided to take a nap for a few hours.

Around 5:30 PM, our guide knocked on our room, inviting us to a brief closing ceremony in the meeting room. We all gathered there, and the owner of Himalayan Hikers joined us. He began by asking about our trekking experience, and each of us shared the memorable moments we had created during the journey.

The owner encouraged us not to be disheartened by the missed summit. Instead, he emphasized a crucial lesson that many trekkers take time to learn—the importance of respecting nature. Drawing from his experiences on 8000-meter summits, where even substantial investments might not guarantee success, he stressed that nature is unparalleled. He shared an incident of an avalanche at 7200 meters, where trekkers prioritized saving a fellow trekker's life over reaching the summit, highlighting the true essence of trekking.

Summarizing, he pointed out that the summit isn't just about reaching the top; it's about the entire journey leading to it. Experiencing extreme weather conditions and snowfall together during this trek would undoubtedly prepare us for future challenges.

Our guide praised the group's performance throughout the trek, and then the certificate distribution commenced. One by one, our names were called, and we were presented with certificates—a moment of pride for all of us. Reaching the base camp and navigating through challenging conditions was no small achievement.

After finishing the closing ceremony, we returned to the shop to return the rental gears and get our deposit back. Once done, I visited a local shop to buy some souvenirs as mementos of this place. Satya joined me, and we purchased keychains, flags, and fridge magnets for our homes.

As we headed back to our hotel, Satya and I decided to plan for tomorrow's journey. All our group members gathered in my room for the discussion.

In the whole group, I was the only one who had visited Uttarakhand before. I suggested that we could go to Rishikesh from Dehradun, which is only a one-hour drive, and Rishikesh is a good place to stay.

I also mentioned the option of Mussoorie, but there isn't much to do there. Everyone agreed with my suggestion that Rishikesh could be explored, and it has better connectivity. Some had flights from Delhi, some had trains from Dehradun, and others had trains from Haridwar. Rishikesh seemed like a good option due to its connectivity to

Dehradun, Haridwar, and even Delhi.

So, Rishikesh it was. I suggested activities like river rafting, bungee jumping, or attending the aarti at Parmarth Ghat in Rishikesh. I also informed them about some excellent cafes in Rishikesh where they could enjoy some really good food.Everyone was very excited to explore Rishikesh.

Everyone went back to their rooms and started packing their luggage. Karthick and I quickly packed our bags and came out from our room. Our guides were waiting for us in the common dining area as dinner was going to be served in a few minutes.

He asked me, "Will you come here again?"

Without giving it a second thought, I replied, "Definitely, I will be coming here again." I also mentioned that I want to go to Everest Base Camp but wasn't sure whether I could do it or not.

My guide reassured me, saying that I would easily be able to do Everest Base Camp as my overall performance is good. He added that our entire group could achieve the same. In fact, my goal was to gain some experience before attempting Everest Base Camp, and that's why I chose Kedarkantha.

Our dinner was ready and served to us. We were all tired from this long journey, so we quickly had our dinner. After eating, we gathered in Sandesh's room to discuss this beautiful journey and how it would change our mindsets.

Given the long day, we decided to sleep early and get some rest. We went to our rooms and slept.

It was around 7:00 AM when we woke up, and by 8:00 AM, we finished our breakfast and checked out of our hotel room. Our guides were waiting for us outside; we hugged them and said goodbye. Even the dog was there to bid us farewell. We all took our seats, and our bus journey towards Dehradun began.

I sat by the window and easily spotted the Kedarkantha peak. I found myself asking the mountain why it hadn't given us a chance to reach the summit. Why did this happen to all of us? We had come from different parts of the country, and I wondered why the mountain treated us this way. These were the questions I silently posed to the peak, holding back tears for not being able to reach the summit.

With tears in my eyes, I lay down to sleep, acknowledging that men do cry; we too have emotions. These tears weren't for any failure but for the hard work we all put in. Lost in these thoughts, I fell asleep without realizing.

Suddenly, I heard a whisper in my ear, saying that the mountain hadn't stopped us from climbing it but had made us stronger to tackle bigger peaks. I woke up abruptly, wondering who was speaking. It was a fleeting dream I had as we left Sankri. I looked out the window, and we had just left the Sankri village. Kedarkantha peak was still visible. This time, I didn't ask anything to the mountain; instead, I smiled and thanked the peak, asking it to make me stronger for many more climbs.

Even though I know it was just a dream, I believe it wasn't just a dream. Kedarkantha, in my belief, whispered in my ear, motivating me to climb more. It's not the end of my climbing journey; it's a new beginning. Without much thought, I decided that my next trek would be Everest Base Camp. I believe I will be able to reach there because this time, the motivation had come from the mountain itself. This is true; Kedarkantha whispers.

www.ingramcontent.com/pod-product-compliance
Lightning Source LLC
Chambersburg PA
CBHW031453150726
47990CB00007B/2735